A Woman's
Unlimited Potential

Book 1

Unlimited! ... Bible Studies for Today's Pentecostal Woman

Arlene Allen, Peggy Musgrove,
Lori O'Dea, & Candy Tolbert

Gospel Publishing House

Springfield, Missouri

02-0275

CONTENTS

FOREWORD

Priscilla is one of the fascinating women of the Bible. She and her husband are mentioned six times in the New Testament and four of these times her name comes first. This would be akin to someone addressing a letter to John and Susan Smith as Mrs. and Mr. Susan and John Smith.

Priscilla's prominent place evidently arises from the fact that she took the lead in presenting the great truths of the gospel. In fact, Acts 18:26 says that Priscilla and Aquila brought the eloquent preacher Apollos to their home and "explained the way of God more accurately." Great expositor that he was, Apollos, compared to Priscilla, was deficient in Bible and gospel knowledge. Tactfully, he was given an opportunity to learn more in the privacy of their home.

What Priscilla did for Apollos, this team of Pentecostal writers now does for you. In this powerful Bible study, they lead you through the lives of eight great women in Scripture, helping you to discover your unlimited potential in Christ Jesus.

Through Esther you discover what it means to be a woman of purpose.

Through the unnamed adulterous woman, you experience what the transformed life is all about. In the young widow Ruth, you see how to develop a maturing lifestyle.

Through Mary of Bethany, you find the keys to being a woman of spiritual passion; and in the elderly widow Anna you understand what it is to live a dedicated life.

Through the political and military leader Deborah, you encounter your life's mission and direction. In Martha, you find the pattern for service. And in Mary of Nazareth, the mother of Jesus, you grow strong in uncompromising commitment to God's perfect will for your life—a will that at times may seem impossible to attain.

But, these writers are not the only ones leading you in this Bible study to discover your unlimited potential. You will have the benefit of studying and discussing with a group of friends or fellow believers. You see, Bible study is meant to be far more than learning a set of facts or formulas for better living. Through small group Bible study we share a common experience as the Holy Spirit guides the discussion. We learn from the insights and examples of others. We are strengthened by their observations and encouraged by their thoughtful comments and helpful prayers.

If you are using this study guide and are not already in a Bible study group, seek out a friend or two and invite them on this journey with you.

Still, beyond the other women whom you will study with—you have an even greater Teacher. The Holy Spirit has promised to reveal Christ and to lead you into all truth.

Thus, this Bible study is for today's Pentecostal woman. We believe that the Holy Spirit brings a deepened reverence for Christ, a sharpened understanding of God's Word, and an empowerment edge which helps us live and witness for Christ more effectively.

Here's what I encourage you to do. At the beginning of each lesson, you are given scriptural references that relate to the woman whose life is represented. Take out your pencil and notepad, and read first what the Bible has to stay about each. Take some moments to "pray over the text." Ask the Holy Spirit, "What do You want to show me here?" Jot down some things that come to your mind as you read the Bible passage.

Then use this Bible study as a way of looking even more deeply at the text of Scripture. Write down your thoughts. Respond to the questions asked. Keep saying to yourself, *What is the Holy Spirit teaching me here? What change is He asking me to make? How is what I am learning helping me to more closely follow Jesus Christ?*

When this Bible study is done, you will be a better person. That process is called "growth in grace."

Someone has said that parents should give their children roots and wings. I think this Bible study will do that for you—roots in God's Word that provide solid grounding for the coming growth in your life and wings to fly into God's future with confidence, joy, and the anointing of the Holy Spirit.

This Bible study has been designed for women of all ages and stations in life. You may be single, married, divorced, or widowed. You may be employed in the marketplace or at home. You may be a pre-believer, a new Christian, or a believer of long-standing. This Bible study is for you!

Now, let's get started!

George O. Wood
General Secretary
General Council of the Assemblies of God

PREFACE

This series of Bible studies was written in response to women and pastors across the United States asking for Pentecostal studies to use in their churches for a group study or as individual study material.

A Woman's Unlimited Potential is a Pentecostal study written by Pentecostal women. This study will be unique to any you have used before because the Pentecostal perspective is written into each lesson. The student will not have to search for the Pentecostal viewpoint—she needs only to embrace it and ask Jesus to help her apply it.

A definition of potential is "something that can develop or become actual." Your potential is unlimited as you understand God's plan for your life.

You may feel you have little potential. Jesus saw a poor widow drop two small coins in the collection and commended her for what He considered a wonderful gift. He took the lunch of a boy and multiplied it to feed thousands. When Jesus' disciples refused to let little children approach Him, He scolded the disciples. Jesus knew those children would grow into men and women. He saw their possibilities. He sees your potential too!

Life is a growing, learning process if you are open to God's leading. He has no illusion of man reaching perfection on this earth. "Being confident of this, that he who began a good work in you will carry it on to completion until the day of Christ Jesus" (Philippians 1:6). The God who began a good work in you continues to perform it throughout your lifetime as you follow Him. He will finish it when you meet Christ face-to-face. God's work on our behalf began long before we were born. His work in us began when we first believed. Now the Holy Spirit lives in us, enabling us to be more like Christ every day.

May these studies be a guide to help you examine your life. May they help you develop to your full potential to become what He has planned.

Arlene Allen
Director, Women's Ministries Department
General Council of the Assemblies of God

INTRODUCTION

HOW TO LEAD A
BIBLE STUDY GROUP

Welcome to the *Unlimited! . . . Bible Studies for Today's Pentecostal Woman* series! You will find these studies to be a great source for biblical guidance in living a Christian life in today's unsteady world, and for learning more about the Holy Spirit's work in your life.

Leading a group in studying these lessons will be challenging and rewarding, as together you discover how to apply God's Word to your life. You may have some questions about leading a Bible study. This section gives direction for answering the why, who, what, where, when, and how questions. Let's look at them individually.

"WHY" QUESTIONS
Why have a Bible study?

The first question you may ask is "Why do we want to have a Bible study?" This series is based on biblical, textual information, meant to be an expository study of what God's Word says on the topics presented in each lesson. Bill Bright, in his book *Discover the Book God Wrote,* says, "The Bible is so interconnected with God that we cannot separate it from His being. In fact, when we read the Bible with the right attitude, God, in the person of the Holy Spirit, joins with our spirit to help us understand it and apply it. The Book comes alive! The words in the Bible have life-changing power."[1]

Bible study group dynamics differ from other small group dynamics. Bible study is not necessarily easy, nor should those studying the Bible try to make it easy. Your main goal for beginning a Bible study should not be for a group to have fellowship, although fellowship will occur. If your main

---

[1]Bill Bright, *Discover the Book God Wrote,* (Wheaton, Ill.: Tyndale House Publishers, Inc., 2003), 5.

purpose is something other than a direct study of God's Word to gain biblical understanding for each member's life today, you may want to consider a different curriculum and format. The main goal of Bible study is to understand the Bible in a more profound way, so it will penetrate deeply into the hearts of those attending.

Bible study differs from traditional small groups in that fellowship can happen before and after the study, but not necessarily during. The Bible study sessions may become intense at times while group members grapple with the life issues presented in these lessons. Lives will be changed as a result of understanding God's Word.

If you combine Bible study with the small group dynamics of worship, prayer, and fellowship, then take that into consideration when planning the length of time for your sessions. Be sure the Bible study time is not crowded out by other activities.

"WHO" QUESTIONS

Who are the study members?

Who are you going to invite to this study? Many possibilities exist for establishing a Bible study group: neighbors (which is beneficial for evangelism), a new convert's study, a working woman's study, or an intergenerational study. Establishing the answer to this question helps answer some of the other questions.

Determine if you are going to establish a limit on the size of the group, and if you are going to allow newcomers to this study once it has started. A recommended size would be no less than four and no more than eleven members. A study group of twelve or more should be divided into smaller groups to facilitate discussion.

Who is the leadership?

Another "who" question is answered by determining who makes up the leadership of this study group. Will more than one person be a facilitator (teacher)? Will you need others in leadership? For example, do you want a group secretary to keep information such as names, addresses, and e-mail addresses of group members, in order to get information to each group member? Do you want a refreshment coordinator or special events coordinator if refreshments or fellowship events are to be a part of your time together? Who will these leaders be? These questions should be determined with the help of your church leadership. The women chosen for these positions need to be mature Christians.

"WHAT" QUESTIONS

The "what" questions will be partially answered when you answer the "who" questions. You may want to consider that these sessions would be valuable for a Sunday School class, or adapted as a couples' Bible study in addition to the suggested women's study groups. Don't limit these studies to just one audience.

Also ask "What will be our format for each session?" These Bible study lessons offer a format that is workable for your study group; however, each group should adapt the lesson components to fit its needs.

"WHERE" QUESTIONS

Where may be determined when you know who is coming. Many settings can be used for these studies, including a room at the church, a restaurant's private room, the lunchroom of an office, a community center, or some-one's home. Once a location is determined, for the strength of the meetings, do not change locations.

"WHEN" QUESTIONS

When will you meet for Bible study? What day will you meet? How long will the meeting last? How long will it take to complete this book of Bible studies?

These studies are planned so that each lesson can be taught in one session, for a total of eight sessions. However, if your group wants to meet for a shorter amount of time each week, the lessons could be taught in two parts, for a total of thirteen to sixteen sessions. One and a half hours is a recommended time for each lesson given in this series, assuming all lesson components are used in each session. Announce a planned start date and a final session date before beginning the unit of study.

The time of day for your meetings, of course, will be determined by the majority of the group attending, and the availability of the space you have chosen. You may want to build in time for fellowship before or after the Bible study; however, remember that it is better to have the study members wanting the meetings to be longer, rather than wishing they were shorter!

"HOW" QUESTIONS

How will you promote your Bible study sessions?

You may want to develop a brochure, place posters in the church hall-ways, ask for bulletin and pulpit announcements, or use any number of creative methods for getting information to potential group members. Be sure potential members understand how and where they can become involved in this study.

Carefully consider these questions and any others you may have to establish the framework for your Bible study. Trust God to be there as you meet together with other women to discover how to apply His Word to your life.

TIPS FOR BEING A BIBLE STUDY GROUP MEMBER

Each Bible study group member is important to the success of these Bible studies. Use these suggestions to help make your time together more meaningful.

- Agree to participate: The more fully each person participates, the more each group member benefits. Agree to study the lesson before the scheduled session, and agree to attend the sessions consistently to share the insight God gives you about each lesson. During discussions, contribute actively without straying from the discussion or dominating the group's time together.
- Respect each other: Through open and honest sharing we encourage one another. We can talk about who we are—our hurts, hopes, joys, and struggles—and what God is doing in us in this study. Each group member has valuable contributions to make to these sessions, and comments of each member should be honored.
- Keep a confidence: What is shared by other study group members during study sessions should stay as part of the group and should not be talked about outside study session time.
- Affirm each other: Affirmation strengthens the body of Christ. We can recognize what is best in other members of this study group and encourage them to develop these qualities as we grow spiritually together.
- Pray: Write down prayer requests of other study members and pray for these requests during the week. Be aware that other study members will be praying for you.

Allow the Holy Spirit to work in your life through these Bible studies. God bless your time together with Him!

TIPS FOR BEING A BIBLE STUDY LEADER

As a leader, you have a determining role in the effectiveness of your Bible study group. Many resources are available to help you. Here are a few tips for some of your responsibilities as a group leader:

Demonstrate personal commitment to Jesus, the Word, and the people you lead.

As a leader, your personal commitment to God is of utmost importance. Leading a group of believers demands a strong personal commitment to God and His Word. Are you growing spiritually as an individual believer? Do you enjoy interacting with people? Do you want to see others grow spiritually? Then you will most likely be able to successfully lead a Bible study group.

Prepare thoroughly in prayer, study, and with a heart for the members of your group.

Use extra study helps if needed, such as Bible concordances, dictionaries, and study Bibles. Write notes in the margin of this study guide to help you facilitate discussion.

Decide before the first session if you will use every component offered in these lessons, or if you will choose only some of the components. See "Understanding and Using the Lesson Components" on page 14 for more information concerning each lesson segment.

The format for teaching these lessons will be interactive lecture, and group reflection and discussion. Be so familiar with the lesson content beforehand that you will be able to keep the group moving forward in the lesson. Ask each study member to read the lesson and write out answers before coming to the session so they will also be ready for discussion.

Facilitate discussion. Know your group and the lesson well enough to carefully select key questions that will generate interaction; resist the temptation to lecture.

Keep the conversations biblically grounded by sticking to the topic of each lesson. Move on to the next question, rather than allowing silence or "down" time, unless the silence is meaningful to the question being considered.

Guard a nurturing environment; encourage uplifting conversation, do not permit gossip, and insist on confidentiality. As possible, involve all study group members in the discussion at some time.

Always invite God's presence in your study sessions. Open and close each session with prayer, not as a formality, but a heartfelt necessity.

UNDERSTANDING AND USING THE LESSON COMPONENTS

You will find consistency in the components of each lesson of this book. An explanation of each component is given to clarify the purpose of each segment, enriching your total study experience.

CATCHING SIGHT
Introduction

The first component, "Catching Sight," directs the reader and study group to the topic of the lesson. Usually an anecdote or true-life story begins each lesson, followed by a brief explanation of the topic. Use these introductions to capture the attention of your group members as they are getting settled. If you are using this series for independent study, this introduction should help focus your mind as you begin.

GETTING FOCUSED
Begin your study by sharing thoughts on the following:

This component of the lesson initiates group discussion on the lesson topic. Break into groups of three to five to discuss the question or statement given in "Getting Focused." If you are studying independently, write down your thoughts on the question or statement. If you are leading a group, ask the group members to look at this question before the session and jot down some thoughts to facilitate discussion.

BIBLE READING

Bible passages selected to accompany each lesson are given in two versions: the New International Version and the *New Living Translation*. These two versions are side by side for easy reference during lesson study.

Shorter Bible readings may be read aloud by an individual or by the group. Longer readings should be read by group members before the session. Portions of the longer reading can be read during study time.

GAINING BIBLICAL INSIGHT

This component is the biblical exposition of the lesson. The pivotal truth of the lesson is given in italics beneath the component section heading. This is the "truth in a nutshell" concerning the topic of the lesson.

REFLECTING HIS IMAGE

This component gives an opportunity for creativity, as well as portraying the truth of the lesson. The Bible woman reflects the incarnation of the lesson's truths, and is given as an example of a life to emulate. This component can be used in several ways:

Individual devotional reading: Ask each group member to read this portion before coming to the study.

Small-group reading: Assign one person to read this component at the appropriate time in class or ask several to women read parts.

Drama: Assign women to portray each character in the Bible story and a narrator. Ask the women to give their practiced dramatic portrayal at an appropriate time in the study. Simple costumes will complete the effect.

Monologue: Request that one woman practice portraying the Bible woman in the lesson, and present a dramatic monologue during the study.

EMBRACING THE PENTECOSTAL PERSPECTIVE
What is the Holy Spirit teaching me?

This perspective of a Pentecostal believer begins by asking, "What is the Holy Spirit teaching me?" We believe the Holy Spirit is a unique Person with a specific ministry in the life of a Christian. The questions raised in this component will help the Pentecostal believer to apply the truths of the lesson in her own life.

INVITING GOD TO CHANGE MY VIEW
What change is God asking me to make?

After interacting with God's Word, seeing it in another woman's life, and discerning how it applies to one's own, there is one more essential step before we can live differently in light of the truth—prayer! This section provides questions that help each participant to go to the heart of the issue, asking God to bring change where it is most needed. Notice that there is always a question provided to open the door for someone to receive Christ as Savior. A prayer is also included as a sample, a starting point, or simply as personal reflection.

JOURNALING

Take a few moments to record your personal insights from the lesson.

Space is given at the end of each lesson and on pages 117–124 for writing down personal thoughts and reflections that transpire during the study of each lesson. The Bible study leader can take time for this in class or request that members complete this on their own time after the session.

Her Unique Purpose

CATCHING SIGHT
Introduction

*D*O YOU REMEMBER the first molded chocolate bunny you received? Do you remember the first bite into one of the long ears and your disappointment in finding it hollow? Empty, hollow, nothing . . . the words ring of disillusionment. Yet this is the life experience of many. Grasping the sweet things—possessions, money, power, and pleasure—they find nothing inside. Life is empty, meaningless, void of purpose.

However, when you know God and follow His guidance, you begin to find purpose for your life. You know you are where God wants you, whether moving or staying in one place. Direction from God is not just for your next big move. He has a purpose in placing you where you are right now. Instead of praying, "God, what do You want me to do next?" ask, "God, what do You want me to do while I'm right here?" Begin to understand God's purpose for your life by discovering what He wants you to do now! This lesson will help you find true purpose in life.

GETTING FOCUSED
Begin your study by considering the following:

Tell of a time when you worked to earn something and achieved it, but had a hollow feeling inside.

Bible Reading
Ecclesiastes 2:17–24; 3:11; 12:13,14

New International Version

2:17 So I hated life, because the work that is done under the sun was grievous to me. All of it is meaningless, a chasing after the wind. 18 I hated all the things I had toiled for under the sun, because I must leave them to the one who comes after me.

19 And who knows whether he will be a wise man or a fool? Yet he will have control over all the work into which I have poured my effort and skill under the sun. This too is meaningless. 20 So my heart began to despair over all my toilsome labor under the sun. 21 For a man may do his work with wisdom, knowledge and skill, and then he must leave all he owns to someone who has not worked for it. This too is meaningless and a great misfortune. 22 What does a man get for all the toil and anxious striving with which he labors under the sun? 23 All his days his work is pain and grief; even at night his mind does not rest. This too is meaningless.

New Living Translation

2:17 So now I hate life because everything done here under the sun is so irrational. Everything is meaningless, like chasing the wind. 18 I am disgusted that I must leave the fruits of my hard work to others.

19 And who can tell whether my successors will be wise or foolish? And yet they will control everything I have gained by my skill and hard work. How meaningless! 20 So I turned in despair from hard work. It was not the answer to my search for satisfaction in this life. 21 For though I do my work with wisdom, knowledge, and skill, I must leave everything I gain to people who haven't worked to earn it. This is not only foolish but highly unfair.

22 So what do people get for all their hard work? 23 Their days of labor are filled with pain and grief; even at night they cannot rest. It is all utterly meaningless.

24 So I decided there is nothing better than to enjoy food and drink

New International Version

24 A man can do nothing better than to eat and drink and find satisfaction in his work. This too, I see, is from the hand of God.

3:11 He has made everything beautiful in its time. He has also set eternity in the hearts of men; yet they cannot fathom what God has done from beginning to end.

12:13 Now all has been heard; here is the conclusion of the matter: Fear God and keep his commandments, for this is the whole [duty] of man. 14 For God will bring every deed into judgment, including every hidden thing, whether it is good or evil.

New Living Translation

and to find satisfaction in work. Then I realized that this pleasure is from the hand of God.

3:11 God has made everything beautiful for its own time. He has planted eternity in the human heart, but even so, people cannot see the whole scope of God's work from beginning to end.

12:13 Here is my final conclusion: Fear God and obey his commands, for this is the duty of every person. 14 God will judge us for everything we do, including every secret thing, whether good or bad.

GAINING BIBLICAL INSIGHT
Discovering God's unique purpose for my life

N othing in life makes sense. It's all meaningless and, believe me, I should
know, I've tried everything and found nothing worthwhile under the
sun."

Does this sound like your neighbor dealing with the frustrations of the
twenty-first century? Many people caught in the conflicts of postmodern
life ask themselves if there is any purpose to it all.

Actually the words are a paraphrase of the words of the ancient King
Solomon. Though he was the richest and wisest of kings, the Book of
Ecclesiastes records his frustrations. A repeated phrase, "under the sun,"
indicates his thoughts were focused primarily on this life, which is the
source of his frustrations. Life viewed only on a horizontal plane does not
make sense.

Scan the first two chapters of the book where Solomon talks about many
things he has found meaningless. **List three or four of them briefly.**

**What was the result of Solomon's efforts according to Ecclesiastes
2:17,18?**

When Solomon begins to view life in another dimension, he moves from
his sense of futility to a sense of purpose. By the end of chapter 2, he begins
to admit God is in control of life (2:24–26).

In chapter 3 Solomon's point of view moves from the natural to the spiritual. He sees that time has purpose and meaning because God is brought into the picture.

In contrast to the futility of men's efforts, how does Solomon see what God does in 3:14?

Gradually we gain insight into Solomon's view that God is the sovereign Creator who has purpose in all He does.

Solomon continues to wrestle with many great questions of life, giving a stirring challenge to young people at the end of the book. This challenge is for all of us no matter what our current age.

"Remember your Creator in the days of your youth, before the days of trouble come and the years approach when you will say, 'I find no pleasure in them' " (Ecclesiastes 12:1).

What difference does seeing God as Creator make in our worldview?

Having acknowledged the Creator God, what is Solomon's final conclusion about the ultimate purpose in life in Ecclesiastes 12:13?

These words, written in Solomon's later years, have one sad note. Solomon did not live by this truth. The Law explicitly forbade Israel's kings to amass fortunes and horses, and to marry foreign wives (Deuteronomy 17:14–17). Solomon did all of these things which later brought problems to Israel.

Jesus and Solomon

Jesus referred to Solomon's wisdom once in His teaching, and made a comparison to himself by saying, "one greater than Solomon is here" (Matthew 12:42).

What contrast do you see between the life of Jesus and what we have learned about Solomon?

Solomon came too late to the realization that what really matters in life is loving reverence for God and living a life of obedience to His will. Jesus, on the other hand, knew His purpose in life from the beginning, and followed that purpose to the end. He is our ultimate example of living a life with meaning.

Solomon, Jesus, and You

Each of us deals with the questions Solomon dealt with. *What is the greatest good? What is the meaning of life?* Our questioning moves from the general to the personal: *What is the purpose of my life?* How do you answer these questions?

Creation implies ownership. If God created human beings, He must have had some purpose for them. The progression of thought moves as before, *If God created me, He must have some purpose for me. When He gave me a new life in Christ, He must have planned how my life should be lived.*

From this point we move to Solomon's conclusion, that we should "Fear God and keep his commandments," which means to live in loving reverence for His authority.

Now we each have choices to make. First we must choose to honor God by receiving Christ into our lives. Then we daily make the choice to seek His purposes and live accordingly.

The Old Testament story of Esther is an example of a woman who understood that God had created her for a specific purpose. Let's take a few minutes and read her story.

REFLECTING HIS IMAGE
Esther (Esther 2:1 to 7:10)

Very few days come into our lives which, when they have come to an end, have changed us forever.

Tired hands gripped the ends of the crimson velvet robe falling loosely around Esther's feet. As her maids secured the heavily jeweled headpiece to her long black hair, Esther thought about Mordecai. Tears stung her deep brown eyes. *Dear brave Mordecai.* She loved him as the father she never knew. Had he followed her instruction to have their people fast and pray? His words from days earlier echoed in her ears.

"Don't think that just because you live in the king's house you're the one Jew who will get out of this alive. If you persist in staying silent at a time like this, help and deliverance will arrive for the Jews from someplace else; but you and your family will be wiped out. Who knows? Maybe you were made queen for just such a time as this."[1]

"For such a time as this" she said, softly now, almost in a whisper. Instinctively she knew he was right. *God must have some divine purpose. I am a Jew. To denounce my heritage and turn my back on my people is unthinkable. Mordecai is right. I have no choice. But then I've never had much choice about my orphaned life. My choices have been limited. Have I made the best of them?* Esther's grace and beauty had captured the heart of a king. Now she must also be courageous. Will it be enough to save her people?

The sun shone and the flowers had an unusually sweet fragrance as Esther began the long walk through the garden to the courtyard of the king's palace. Three maids followed closely, heads slightly bent, tears filling their eyes. The fate of their queen would be known shortly. To approach King Xerxes without being summoned meant certain death. Would he save

---

[1]Esther 4:13,14, *The Message.*

her by holding out his scepter to her?

I've never confronted evil head-on, Esther thought. Even now, remembering Haman's plot to murder the entire Jewish race caused her hands to feel icy and numb. *He must be stopped,* she reasoned. *Even though I am queen, if I die today, I die.* A determined faith carried her, until she stood erectly facing the king's throne room. Ten seconds. Thirty seconds. A mouth dry as dust. Legs weak as willow branches. Yet with courage and a deliberate walk, she entered the very presence of the king.

Their eyes met and at that moment she saw on the face of her king a look she had come to know and admire. King Xerxes loved and cherished her. He held out the golden scepter. Esther approached slowly in silence and touched the tip of the scepter.

"What is it, my queen?" the king asked. "What is troubling you? What would you like? Name it and it is yours, even up to half the kingdom."

Suddenly, Esther felt the fear inside her melt away as she cleared her voice to speak. Time to seize a divine moment. Time for a request she knew he would not refuse. Time for such a time as this. "Your Majesty," she said, "come today with Haman to a dinner I have prepared for you."

Days later, she smiled to herself and pondered what God had done through her. Haman executed. Her people spared and Mordecai honored. And now she treasured a private moment, as she looked to the light of the heavens in humble adoration. The view from her window was especially beautiful as millions of stars seemed to sing in the brilliant evening sky.

Thank You, God, for courage and strength and confidence, she prayed, *and for the knowledge that You gave my life purpose . . . for such a time as this.*

EMBRACING THE PENTECOSTAL PERSPECTIVE
What is the Holy Spirit teaching me?

You have simple choices to make after encountering Solomon and Esther. You could despise King Solomon because he did not use the wisdom given him. Or you could learn with Solomon that when God is in control, life has purpose. You could admire Esther or identify with her. If you simply admire her, you may be tempted to put her on a pedestal as more beautiful or more privileged than yourself. On the other hand, if you choose to identify with Esther—a woman desiring to do God's will with talent, opportunities and Spirit-empowerment—you could discover world-changing purpose.

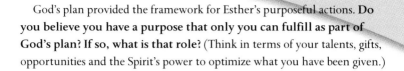

God's plan provided the framework for Esther's purposeful actions. **Do you believe you have a purpose that only you can fulfill as part of God's plan? If so, what is that role?** (Think in terms of your talents, gifts, opportunities and the Spirit's power to optimize what you have been given.)

Esther and Solomon both used prayer as a simple means of finding God's purpose for their lives. **How do you remove distractions and get clarity for hearing God?**

Do you tend to seek everyone's opinion but God's about direction for your life? What is the difference between opinion-gathering and asking prayer for guidance?

How do you maintain an attitude of humility, rather than pre-sumption in your prayer life?

Share an experience in which the Holy Spirit has given you bold-ness to speak or act on God's behalf.

What do you need wisdom for in your life right now? Have you asked Him for it? (James 1:5)

Spirit-empowered living requires a unique tension in our lives between humility and boldness. Esther embodies both. She demonstrates humility by not presuming that her position entitles her to anything (4:11). Such humil-ity creates a capacity for boldness, enabling her to approach the throne uninvited, an act punishable by death (5:1). On the other hand, Solomon did not live up to the purpose he was called to fulfill.

INVITING GOD TO CHANGE MY VIEW

What change is God asking me to make?

God has a unique purpose for your life. Do you need Him to clarify yours? This kind of understanding comes through a relationship with Jesus Christ. Have you invited Jesus to forgive your sins and be your Lord?

Perhaps you know what God is calling you to do, but you lack the courage or understanding to proceed. Do you need to be filled with the Spirit? Do you need to be refilled? Do you need to repent for a lack of humility or disobedience to God's call? Do you lack boldness? What specific areas of your life do you need to ask God to direct?

Prayer

Father, thank You for giving me a unique purpose. Sometimes I don't see it right away, but I want to understand what my purpose is. Help me remember that I don't have to do anything on my own. Teach me to rely on Your Spirit for understanding and courage. I want to know the joy of fulfilling Your purpose, for living like Jesus, and being part of Your perfect plan. Thank You for allowing me to partner with You, Lord. Amen.

JOURNALING

Take a few moments to record your personal insights from the lesson.

Her Transformed Life

CATCHING SIGHT
Introduction

*D*URING A COLD, colorless winter, death seems to reign in nature until suddenly, on a seemingly lifeless branch, pale pink buds appear. Soon, the tulip magnolia tree blossoms and nature's transformation begins. Winter's pale death gives way to the vibrant life of spring.

The transformation of nature in spring is an annual illustration of the new life Christ offers to those who come to Him. The Bible describes the transformation from sin to salvation as passing from death to life. The new life Christ offers is as fresh as springtime.

Major changes begin in our hearts as God works on our attitudes, beliefs, and desires. These inner changes lead to outward actions. Our inner world may be turned upside down when we are transformed by Christ. The gospel is not about the business of merely improving programs and encouraging good conduct, but of dynamically transforming lives. Take courage and realize that as you submit to Him daily, your life will be transformed.

GETTING FOCUSED
Begin your study by considering the following:

Give your testimony about the transformation God brought to your life when you became a Christian.

Bible Reading
Ephesians 2:1–13; 18–22

New International Version

1 As for you, you were dead in your transgressions and sins, 2 in which you used to live when you followed the ways of this world and of the ruler of the kingdom of the air, the spirit who is now at work in those who are disobedient. 3 All of us also lived among them at one time, gratifying the cravings of our sinful nature and following its desires and thoughts. Like the rest, we were by nature objects of wrath. 4 But because of his great love for us, God, who is rich in mercy, 5 made us alive with Christ even when we were dead in transgressions—it is by grace you have been saved. 6 And God raised us up with Christ and seated us with him in the heavenly realms in Christ Jesus, 7 in order that in the coming ages he might show the incomparable riches of his grace, expressed in his kindness to us in Christ Jesus. 8 For it is by grace you have been saved, through faith—and this not from yourselves, it is the gift of God—9 not by works, so that no one can boast. 10 For we are God's workmanship, created in Christ Jesus to do good works, which God prepared in advance for us to do.

11 Therefore, remember that formerly you who are Gentiles by birth

New Living Translation

1 Once you were dead, doomed forever because of your many sins. 2 You used to live just like the rest of the world, full of sin, obeying Satan, the mighty prince of the power of the air. He is the spirit at work in the hearts of those who refuse to obey God. 3 All of us used to live that way, following the passions and desires of our evil nature. We were born with an evil nature, and we were under God's anger just like everyone else.

4 But God is so rich in mercy, and he loved us so very much, 5 that even while we were dead because of our sins, he gave us life when he raised Christ from the dead. (It is only by God's special favor that you have been saved!) 6 For he raised us from the dead along with Christ, and we are seated with him in the heavenly realms—all because we are one with Christ Jesus. 7 And so God can always point to us as examples of the incredible wealth of his favor and kindness toward us, as shown in all he has done for us through Christ Jesus.

8 God saved you by his special favor when you believed. And you can't take credit for this; it is a gift from God. 9 Salvation is not a

New International Version

and called "uncircumcised" by those who call themselves "the circumcision" (that done in the body by the hands of men)—12 remember that at that time you were separate from Christ, excluded from citizenship in Israel and foreigners to the covenants of the promise, without hope and without God in the world. 13 But now in Christ Jesus you who once were far away have been brought near through the blood of Christ.

18 For through him we both have access to the Father by one Spirit.

19 Consequently, you are no longer foreigners and aliens, but fellow citizens with God's people and members of God's household, 20 built on the foundation of the apostles and prophets, with Christ Jesus himself as the chief cornerstone. 21 In him the whole building is joined together and rises to become a holy temple in the Lord. 22 And in him you too are being built together to become a dwelling in which God lives by his Spirit.

New Living Translation

reward for the good things we have done, so none of us can boast about it. 10 For we are God's masterpiece. He has created us anew in Christ Jesus, so that we can do the good things he planned for us long ago.

11 Don't forget that you Gentiles used to be outsiders by birth. You were called "the uncircumcised ones" by the Jews, who were proud of their circumcision, even though it affected only their bodies and not their hearts. 12 In those days you were living apart from Christ. You were excluded from God's people, Israel, and you did not know the promises God had made to them. You lived in this world without God and without hope. 13 But now you belong to Christ Jesus. Though you once were far away from God, now you have been brought near to him because of the blood of Christ.

18 Now all of us, both Jews and Gentiles, may come to the Father through the same Holy Spirit because of what Christ has done for us.

19 So now you Gentiles are no longer strangers and foreigners. You are citizens along with all of God's holy people. You are members of God's family. 20 We are his house, built on the foundation of the apostles and the prophets. And the cornerstone is Christ Jesus himself. 21 We who believe are carefully joined together, becoming a holy

New Living Translation
temple for the Lord. 22 Through
him you Gentiles are also joined
together as part of this dwelling
where God lives by his Spirit.

GAINING BIBLICAL INSIGHT
Choosing life in Christ instead of death in sin

*Y*ou have heard the question "Which came first, the chicken or the egg?"
Eggs come from chickens and chickens from eggs but how did the cycle
begin? Our answer to this seemingly insignificant question reveals our basic
view of how the world came into being.

A similar question is "Which comes first, salvation or good works?" Are
we saved because we live good lives, or do we live good lives because we are
saved? Our answer reveals our position on eternal principles. Christianity's
answer sets it apart from most other world religions.

From Death to Life
Read Ephesians 2:8,9. According to these verses, how are we saved?

What is definitely not the means of our salvation?

Good works can never earn eternal salvation; this would make our salvation a product of our own efforts. Instead, Paul says we are "God's workmanship, created in Christ Jesus." When we came to Him as repentant sinners, He totally transformed our lives. Because of His purpose for us, we now engage in good works which glorify Him.

No amount of effort could earn passage from our sinful lives into the presence of a holy God. However, God reaches down in mercy and offers us salvation by faith. To explain the futility of self-effort for salvation, Paul employs the image of death and resurrection.

In verse 1, how does he describe our condition before we were saved?

Whose control and influence were we responding to (verse 2)?

By referring to the sinful person as dead, Paul shows the futility of self-effort for salvation. We can do nothing to save ourselves, anymore than a dead person can put forth effort to change his circumstance. In this sinful condition, steps for self-improvement are like sprucing up a dead person with a new hairstyle and change of clothes. If the sin issue has not been dealt with, we are still dead in our relationship with God.

Christ's resurrection from the dead illustrates our new life in Him. Because of His mercy and God's grace, we are transformed by the resurrection power of God. In appreciation we give Him our lives, desiring that everything we do will bring honor to Him.

From Aliens to Citizens

Read Ephesians 2:11–13. Here Paul employs another comparison to further our understanding of our new position in Christ. While we were in sin, we were separated from God, aliens to His kingdom. Now we have citizenship in the heavenly kingdom and membership in the family of God.

How does Paul describe our former condition in verse 12?

What change do we experience when we become Christians (verse 13)?

As members of the family of God, we now have access in prayer to God by the work of Jesus Christ and through the enabling power of the Holy Spirit (verse 18). God hears our prayers, not because of our righteousness, but because of our relationship with Him.

From Separation to Connection

Paul also illustrates the new relationship we have in the family of God with the metaphor of a building. He talks about our separation from God and from each other, and contrasts that disconnectedness to the structural unity of a building.

Read Ephesians 2:19–22. **On what foundation is this building built?**

Who is the "chief cornerstone"?

This chapter shows the steps God takes to bring each of us into fellowship with Him. First, He transforms us into new creatures in Christ Jesus. Second, He brings us into relationship with himself and other believers in Christian community. His Spirit works in our lives individually, while He builds us collectively into the kingdom of God.

The one thing He does not do is choose for us. He leaves to us the choice as to how we will live our lives. After our initial choice to accept Christ, we make choices daily to ignore or yield to the teaching of God's Word and the gentle working of the Holy Spirit who wants to lead us to maturity in Christ.

Jesus offered this clear choice to the adulterous woman. Her story illustrates for us the possibility of radical transformation from a sinful life to walking in the forgiveness of Christ. Let's hear her story.

REFLECTING HIS IMAGE
The Adulterous Woman (John 8:3–11)

Though people say I'm young, I've already experienced more of life than most of my sisters and cousins. I haven't married. Haven't had any children of my own. Don't see much use I guess. For a long time, I searched and searched for a special kind of love. Do you understand what I mean by special? It's the kind of love that offers fulfillment, completeness, and a future— an unconditional love you might say. My search led me down a path of abuse, disgrace, heartache, and virtually one broken relationship after another. I'm now known throughout the region as one of *those* women.

You can imagine my shame and disgrace as I was dragged by my hair and hurled at the feet of the Pharisees. I was brought to the middle of the temple court with nowhere to hide and no one to defend me. You should have seen that angry mob of people with rocks raised to pummel me with their judgment. Believe me, I know the Law. According to the teaching of Moses, both parties caught in the act of adultery are to be stoned. But they left *him* back at his place. I don't have proof, but I believe my accusers set me up.

Let me ask you something. Who would you rather face if you were caught red-handed: God Almighty or human accusers?[1] Yesterday, I faced my human accusers; I didn't know I was also going to face God.

He was there, sitting in the temple courtyard. I stood before Him; my head bent low, ashamed, half-naked, trying to cover myself. And He looked right through me with the most amazing eyes I have ever seen! At that moment, He stepped closer. Ignoring the questions from the angry crowd, He knelt down. Using His finger, He began to write something on the ground. They kept at Him, badgering Him. Slowly and deliberately, the Man straightened up and said, "The sinless one among you, go first: Throw the stone."[2]

The courtyard became silent as one by one my accusers dropped their stones and walked away. I still stood, trembling and alone. For the first time in years, I felt tears sting my eyes! This man Jesus stood up and spoke to me. "Woman, where are they? Does no one condemn you?"

"No one, Sir," I said.

"Neither do I condemn you," said Jesus. "Go now and leave your life of sin."[3]

---

[1] *Voices of Faith,* 1366.
[2] John 8:7, *The Message.*
[3] John 8:11.

Yesterday, I was face-to-face with God. Today, I can face my future. I never want to return to my former life. Not because I am afraid of being punished or even dying. But because for the first time I have found that special kind of compassionate love I had been searching for. Jesus liberated me with His forgiveness of my sin. This is my chance for a new beginning, a fresh start, and a clean slate. Now my life can be transformed.

EMBRACING THE PENTECOSTAL PERSPECTIVE
What is the Holy Spirit teaching me?

Wanting a good thing but going after it in the wrong way is an experience nearly everyone can relate to. We learned from Ephesians that we were all dead in sin when we followed the ways of this world. Thankfully, everyone can share the adulterous woman's testimony. God changes people! No matter what the sin, how terrible the past, or how deep the hurt, the Lord offers total transformation through the power of the Spirit. From Ephesians we know it is by grace, through faith, we are saved.

Our study in Ephesians and the testimony of the adulterous woman (John 8:3–11) help us understand three ways the Holy Spirit transforms our lives: a new perspective that enables change, truth that makes us alive, and joy that accompanies newness of life.

Jesus told His disciples the Holy Spirit would teach us "all things" (John 14:26). He helps us recognize both the good and the bad. That's what He did for the adulterous woman. She saw the awfulness of sin in her life, while simultaneously catching a glimpse of the Savior. Her perspective changed, like passing from death to life.

Describe the moment you saw your sinful behavior for what it was. Be sure to include how the Spirit brought this insight (e.g., the comment of a friend, the response of a child, or a new understanding of Scripture).

When did you first encounter God's grace reaching out to you, revealing Jesus' love?

A new perspective gained through the work of the Spirit prepares our hearts to receive the truth, and—in the pivotal moment in which we accept it—to experience miraculous deliverance. The Ephesians 2 passage shows us that accepting the truth of God's grace in sending His Son makes us alive. When Jesus said, "The truth will set you free" (John 8:32), He gave a concise description of the transformation process. Truth precedes freedom. No detours can take us around truth to freedom.

Envision yourself in the crowd surrounding the adulterous woman. Imagine the adrenaline pumping through your veins and the feel of a sizeable rock in your hand. **What causes you to change your perspective, release your grip and walk away?**

Do you need to be made alive in Christ today? Do you need His truth to set you free?

"If anyone is in Christ, he is a new creation; the old has gone, the new has come!" (2 Corinthians 5:17). The exuberance heard in these words captures the sense of joy that accompanies the Spirit's transforming work. Moving from old sinful ways is not just a good idea or a command; it is life-changing, thrilling, and continuously interesting! Earlier in this lesson we learned that when we leave the ways of the world, we become a dwelling place for God's Spirit.

Have your actions changed as a result of becoming a dwelling place for God's Spirit?

Do you believe that the newness of life in Christ can and should always be present in your journey with the Lord, no matter how long you've been following Him? If not, why not? If so, how?

INVITING GOD TO CHANGE MY VIEW

What change is God asking me to make?

Transformation is one of God's greatest promises. To be stuck in a perpetual cycle of wanting new life, yet holding to the ways of the world (Ephesians 2:2), is in direct contradiction to the life in the Spirit that God intends for us. He desires to make our hearts a dwelling place for the Spirit. Today, we want to pray for transformation in our lives.

Have you been introduced to Jesus yet? Do you need to bring sin out into the open, so that God can deal with it? Would you like the Spirit to create the assurance that you are a citizen of the heavenly kingdom? Is the Spirit of God truly dwelling in your heart? Do you need more joy in your relationship with the Lord? Is there a specific area in your life in which you need God to accelerate His metamorphosis?

Prayer

Precious Lord, thank You for bringing me new life when I was dead in sin. Thank You for giving me new hope. I believe that You want to continue Your transforming work in my life. Make my life a dwelling place for Your Spirit. Today, I'm trusting You to bring positive change to my life. Help me keep my eyes on You instead of my accuser. Forgive me for hiding behind my own self-righteousness instead of standing freely in Your grace. Let me be submissive to Your Spirit—seeing what You want me to see, learning what You want me to learn, running in the newness of life. I love You, Lord. In Jesus' name, Amen.

JOURNALING

Take a few moments to record your personal insights from the lesson.

Her
Maturing Lifestyle

CATCHING SIGHT
Introduction

WHAT DO YOU do before you start a journey? Most likely, you get a map and choose your route, plan what clothes and other items to take with you, determine how long you'll be gone, and what you want to do when you arrive at your destination.

But before anything else, you have to decide to take the journey in the first place. It requires an act of your conscious will. The Christian's journey to maturity requires the same act of will. We decide to become a Christian, then commit to the journey of maturing in Christ.

A familiar Mother Goose rhyme says: "Pussycat, pussycat, where have you been? I've been to London to visit the queen. Pussycat, pussycat, what did you there? I frightened a little mouse under her chair." Like that cat, Christians sometimes settle for petty involvements and trivial pursuits—chasing mice—when the journey could have meant spending time with royalty, with the King!

God could instantly make you a mature believer, but He chooses to help you gradually, teaching you one lesson at a time. Rather than expecting instant spiritual maturity and solutions to all your problems, slow down and work one step at a time, trusting God to make up the difference between where you should be and where you are now. A rewarding part of any journey is looking back to see how far you've come. On this road to maturity, you'll see how God transforms your life in miraculous ways.

GETTING FOCUSED

Begin your study by considering the following:

List an attribute you admire in others that you want to have as part of your life.

Bible Reading

Ephesians 4:17–32

New International Version

17 So I tell you this, and insist on it in the Lord, that you must no longer live as the Gentiles do, in the futility of their thinking. 18 They are darkened in their understanding and separated from the life of God because of the ignorance that is in them due to the hardening of their hearts. 19 Having lost all sensitivity, they have given themselves over to sensuality so as to indulge in every kind of impurity, with a continual lust for more.

20 You, however, did not come to know Christ that way. 21 Surely you heard of him and were taught in him in accordance with the truth that is in Jesus. 22 You were taught, with regard to your former way of life, to put off your old self, which is being corrupted by its deceitful desires; 23 to be made new in the attitude of your minds; 24 and to put on the new self, created to be like God in true righteousness and holiness.

25 Therefore each of you must

New Living Translation

17 With the Lord's authority let me say this: Live no longer as the ungodly do, for they are hopelessly confused. 18 Their closed minds are full of darkness; they are far away from the life of God because they have shut their minds and hardened their hearts against him. 19 They don't care anymore about right and wrong, and they have given themselves over to immoral ways. Their lives are filled with all kinds of impurity and greed.

20 But that isn't what you were taught when you learned about Christ. 21 Since you have heard all about him and have learned the truth that is in Jesus, 22 throw off your old evil nature and your former way of life, which is rotten through and through, full of lust and deception. 23 Instead, there must be a spiritual renewal of your thoughts and attitudes. 24 You must display a new nature because you are a new person, created in God's likeness—righteous, holy, and true.

New International Version

put off falsehood and speak truth-fully to his neighbor, for we are all members of one body. 26 "In your anger do not sin": Do not let the sun go down while you are still angry, 27 and do not give the devil a foothold. 28 He who has been steal-ing must steal no longer, but must work, doing something useful with his own hands, that he may have something to share with those in need.

29 Do not let any unwholesome talk come out of your mouths, but only what is helpful for building others up according to their needs, that it may benefit those who listen. 30 And do not grieve the Holy Spirit of God, with whom you were sealed for the day of redemption. 31 Get rid of all bitterness, rage and anger, brawling and slander, along with every form of malice. 32 Be kind and compassionate to one another, forgiving each other, just as in Christ God forgave you.

New Living Translation

25 So put away all falsehood and "tell your neighbor the truth" because we belong to each other. 26 And "don't sin by letting anger gain control over you." Don't let the sun go down while you are still angry, 27 for anger gives a mighty foothold to the Devil.

28 If you are a thief, stop stealing. Begin using your hands for honest work, and then give generously to others in need. 29 Don't use foul or abusive language. Let everything you say be good and helpful, so that your words will be an encourage-ment to those who hear them.

30 And do not bring sorrow to God's Holy Spirit by the way you live. Remember, he is the one who has identified you as his own, guar-anteeing that you will be saved on the day of redemption.

31 Get rid of all bitterness, rage, anger, harsh words, and slander, as well as all types of malicious behav-ior. 32 Instead, be kind to each other, tenderhearted, forgiving one another, just as God through Christ has forgiven you.

GAINING BIBLICAL INSIGHT
Transforming my life by maturing in Christ

What changes would you make if you moved from a cold climate to a warm region? Winter apparel for lighter clothing? Snow blowers for fans? Ice skates for tennis rackets? The change in climate would greatly affect your life.

Becoming a Christian can be compared to making such a radical change. As new creatures in Christ, we leave some things behind and put on others appropriate to our new life. In Ephesians Paul makes several comparisons between the two ways of life.

Your New Life in Christ

Ephesians 4:17–19 describes the Ephesians' previous life. **What are some characteristics of that lifestyle?**

Some people may turn to the Lord from a similiar life style. Those who accept Christ when very young may be spared these things. Others may have turned to the Lord from a lifestyle similar to the Ephesians. Either way, the saving grace of God reaches us in our sinful condition, calling us to new life in Christ.

Read Ephesians 4:20–24. Paul shows the difference in the two ways of living by using the imagery of a person taking off worn-out clothing and putting on new clothes.

How does he describe the way we used to be?

Your Maturing Life in Christ

YOUR CONVERSATION

God offers us a "new self," making us "new in the attitude" of our minds. Read Ephesians 4:25–32. Note how interrelated our spiritual lives are to everyday living. Paul describes in one breath how we think and speak, how we spend our time and money, and the importance of maintaining the presence of the Holy Spirit. Our Christian life is not compartmentalized into separate sections. Being a Christian affects our total way of living.

Paul talks first about how the new attitude affects our speech. **What is the first characteristic of speech Paul mentions?**

On what occasions might someone not be truthful? Is this ever justifiable?

Earlier in the chapter (verse 15), Paul challenges the Ephesians to speak the truth "in love," dealing not only with the content of speech but the attitude in which we express ourselves. **How does love affect truth when we speak?**

What additional characteristic does Paul list in verse 29?

Sometimes truth is not spoken lovingly, and this does not benefit the listener. Sometimes in an attempt to be loving or kind, we withhold part of the truth which does not benefit the listener either. The conversation of a maturing Christian should pass the threefold test of being true, loving, and beneficial to the hearer.

OUR EMOTIONS

Next, Paul discusses emotional control which often affects the way we speak.

Life brings frustrations and disappointments to which we may respond with varying degrees of anger from irritation to outbursts of rage. **What does Paul say we should do with anger in verse 26? What is the purpose for this?**

Read verse 31 where Paul talks about the forms of anger. **What further instruction about anger does he give in this verse? Is this the same as putting off the old self which he talked about earlier?**

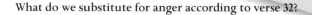

What do we substitute for anger according to verse 32?

Whose example should we follow according to verse 32?

Paul is teaching these new Christians that everything about their life is affected by their relationship with the Lord. What they say, think, and feel should be an expression of the new life within them. While he couches the instructions in terms of what they do, like putting off an old garment, his teaching includes that they are a new creation in Christ Jesus. The new life is within them, and they make the choice to let that life grow into Christian maturity.

OUR TIME AND MONEY

In verse 28, Paul covers another significant part of life, how we spend time and money. He is writing to a group of people for whom stealing had been a livelihood. Now, he is telling them to change from that lifestyle and work for their money. In this one statement, he deals with life at the very basic level of existence and dignifies the daily work we do for a living.

Notice the huge change they are making in lifestyle. Formerly, they took from others for themselves. Now, their time should be given to working so they can give to others. That's a 180-degree turn in lifestyle.

An important principle of Christian economics is found in this verse. **What does the average person who has a job do with surplus funds after providing for daily needs?**

What does this verse say a believer should do with surplus funds?

One gains to have, the other gains to give. Working diligently and giving generously are two characteristics of a maturing Christian.

Your New Life in the Christian Community

In all of Paul's instructions to new believers, he includes reasons beyond themselves for making changes of lifestyle. How we live affects not only ourselves but others around us. This teaching is another reminder that Christians live in community. Let's look at each of the areas we just studied and see how our behavior affects other people.

Why do we speak truthfully, according to verse 25?

What effect does untruthful speech have on relationships?

How does unresolved anger affect relationships in the Christian community, according to verse 27?

What effect does unwholesome speech have according to verses 29 and 30?

Who will benefit when Christians have a clear understanding of Christian economic principles?

The picture Paul paints here is of mature Christians living in harmony in Christian community. Their needs are met because they are working. They share their surplus with any who are unable to work. They speak to each other truthfully in love. When they are frustrated with each other, they deal with anger promptly and appropriately. Their relationships are marked by the kindness of Christ.

Your New Life in Partnership with God

In presenting this ideal, Paul recognizes human weaknesses. He makes it plain that we will have to work at some things if we want to attain Christian maturity.

However, we do not work in our own strength but we are helped by the triune God. When we have difficulty in relationships, we can forgive because we remember we have been forgiven by God the Father, because of Christ.

We gain help also from the Holy Spirit, according to verse 30, who has "sealed" us for "the day of redemption." When we yield to Him, rather than do things which grieve Him, He is our helper in living a mature Christian life.

The life changes we make as maturing believers can be compared to the changes a person makes when moving from one climate or culture to another. The Bible story of Ruth relates the changes she made when she moved from Moab to Bethlehem. Let's listen to her story.

REFLECTING HIS IMAGE
Ruth (Ruth 1)

They tried their best to console me the day my husband died. Cold rain pelted my clothes. My religious Moabite family crowded around me at the burial, shielding me from intruders and the elements. I remember two thoughts about the long, wet walk home that morning. It was hard to breathe. And I felt utterly alone. Except for Naomi.

Do you have a friendship you know will last a lifetime? Do you trust someone completely with everything you have, everything you are? When I married my husband several years ago, I did not know that when I gave my life to the God of Israel I was also deciding to trust His people. That's what *she* taught me.

Often, in the face of past disappointments, I felt I had adequate reason to give up trusting God. What fair-minded person would have blamed me for taking my future into my own hands that day at my husband's grave? I'm young, widowed, with no land and no way to earn a living. I was not born into the faith of my husband and felt no natural part of it. Yet, returning to my father's house was unthinkable.

Some in my family scoffed at my decision to leave Moab with my mother-in-law, reminding me that Naomi was not the most engaging friend to me in the beginning. I'll admit there were days when I felt ignored and neglected. But I saw past Naomi's disillusion and bitterness as I reminded myself that she too faced many changes in her life. Changes which caused her to see only a depressing and empty future.

God was working in her life despite her discouragement. Our journey began. Day-by-day we learned to depend on God for our survival.

"Are you all right?" I asked one afternoon when she was unusually quiet.

"Fine," she replied. "I'm fine."

I knew better because I know her. After a momentary silence, she spoke her mind, insisting firmly that my sister-in-law and I turn back and go home to live with our mothers. Naomi cried bitterly, opening a window of sorrow and pain and motherly love. I stood my ground. She knew I meant business when I said, "Don't force me to leave you; don't make me go home. Where you go, I go; and where you live, I'll live. Your people are my people, your God is my god; where you die, I'll die, and that's where I'll be buried, so help me God—not even death itself is going to come between us!"[1]

---

[1]Ruth 1:16,17, *The Message.*

Naomi looked up and smiled, a smile of assurance. I hold a permanent place in her family. She is my trusted friend. And, unlike my sister-in-law Orpah, I will not be dissuaded. I am committed to this relationship, no matter what!

I must be on my way now. We've still so much to do. But before I go, may I encourage you today? God sees beyond heartache and struggle. He will never abandon you, even when you feel you are all alone. We will arrive in Bethlehem in a few days, mother-in-law and daughter-in-law, one a Hebrew and one a Moabite, journeying together. And who knows what unexpected blessings lay ahead. Surely the best is yet to come!

EMBRACING THE PENTECOSTAL PERSPECTIVE

What is the Holy Spirit teaching me?

Thanks to God's Word, we know the rest of Ruth's story. We know what lay ahead of her as she traveled to an unknown land. She was going to experience God's amazing provision and meet her new husband. She would also be blessed with a son and eventually find her way into the family tree of the Lord Jesus Christ (Matthew 1:5). Not bad for a woman who had lost almost everything.

If only there weren't so many unknowns along the way. If only the path from point A to point B were always straight and uncluttered. If only there were a way to guarantee instant spiritual maturity.

The journey with Christ cannot be confined to a book, a class, a method, or even a length of time. Spiritual growth is a continuous, divine act of the Holy Spirit in which we are called to be active participants.

Let's look at a few key components of such growth. Trust is the first. Ruth demonstrates enormous confidence in Naomi by agreeing to stick with her. She didn't know her mother-in-law's country or customs; she simply believed that she was to follow. We demonstrate our trust in God when we accept the new life He offers, and then begin walking with Him on the journey to maturity.

Why do some find it hard to trust God with everything in their lives all the time? What obstacles keep some of us from trusting God?

Self-sacrifice is another necessity for spiritual maturity. Sometimes maturity calls for a complete turn of lifestyle as Ruth demonstrated in leaving Moab and heading for Bethlehem. Christians are called to live in a place of dependence—upon Christ and other believers. A true sign of growth is the ability to put others' interests before our own.

According to Ephesians 4, what should Christians be willing to give to others?

Where have you given your time this week?

Who have you served this week in a truly self-sacrificing way?

Ruth may have been tempted to turn back to Moab at some point in her journey. Growing in Christ requires persevering in Him. Perseverance requires the stamina of the Spirit, the One called alongside the believer. If we are willing to rely on the Spirit daily, we'll find no end to our potential in Christ.

What have you quit too soon?

In what area of your life (it's all spiritual, by the way, including your diet and exercise) do you need the Spirit's discipline?

INVITING GOD TO CHANGE MY VIEW
What change is God asking me to make?

Throughout Scripture, in both its character sketches and teaching portions, writers give brilliant pictures of what a mature believer looks and acts like. Dismissing this view is a dangerous folly. Being inspired to grow into it is, indeed, a worthwhile endeavor.

What is the most important, yet most difficult, thing you need to do to grow in Christ? How is your prayer life? Are you spending time in the Word, in worship, and in fellowship with other believers? Does your speech reflect a maturity in Christ? How about your time and giving? Do you reflect Jesus more today than you did last year? Are you crowding the throne of your heart—putting yourself in control? Is Jesus Christ the Lord of your life?

Prayer
God, I want to grow. I'm tired of the same old habits, same old mistakes, same existence. I want to experience the excitement of trying new things for You. You know me. You know that my fear and failure to follow through on good intentions has hindered me in the past. Teach me to get out of the way and trust You to nurture new growth in me. Help me to stick with You through the painful and awkward stages that sometimes accompany growth. Thank You for being my patient Teacher, my ever-loving Father. Thank You for the Holy Spirit, who helps me on the journey to maturity. In Jesus' name, Amen.

JOURNALING

Take a few moments to record your personal insights from the lesson.

Her Dedicated Living

CATCHING SIGHT

Introduction

*O*NE SUNDAY MORNING, a pioneer preacher in a small Western town paused to collect the offering. As the preacher prayed for the offering, he asked God to bless those who had provision to give, and those who didn't. When the offering plate passed by a certain church member, he put the plate on the floor in the aisle, then stood in the plate.

The preacher was so surprised, he was speechless. The entire congregation shared his astonishment. Then the church member explained. "I have no money" he said, "so I give myself."

The Church still needs the gifts of gold and silver. But what about the Christian who wants to dedicate her total being to Christ? Who can tell the work to be accomplished through the life of one completely and totally dedicated, through the work of the Holy Spirit, to Christ and His work? You may not have silver or gold, but you do have yourself and all that you are. Are you willing to be like that church member and present your total self in service to God?

GETTING FOCUSED

Begin your study by sharing thoughts on these questions:

What reasons might keep us from being totally dedicated Christians? Do you think the reasons are valid?

Bible Reading

Romans 12:1,2; 9–21

New International Version

1 Therefore, I urge you, brothers, in view of God's mercy, to offer your bodies as living sacrifices, holy and pleasing to God—this is your spiritual act of worship. 2 Do not conform any longer to the pattern of this world, but be transformed by the renewing of your mind. Then you will be able to test and approve what God's will is—his good, pleasing and perfect will.

9 Love must be sincere. Hate what is evil; cling to what is good. 10 Be devoted to one another in brotherly love. Honor one another above yourselves. 11 Never be lacking in zeal, but keep your spiritual fervor, serving the Lord. 12 Be joyful in hope, patient in affliction, faithful in prayer. 13 Share with God's people who are in need. Practice hospitality.

14 Bless those who persecute you; bless and do not curse. 15 Rejoice with those who rejoice; mourn with those who mourn.

New Living Translation

1 And so, dear brothers and sisters, I plead with you to give your bodies to God. Let them be a living and holy sacrifice—the kind he will accept. When you think of what he has done for you, is this too much to ask? 2 Don't copy the behavior and customs of this world, but let God transform you into a new person by changing the way you think. Then you will know what God wants you to do, and you will know how good and pleasing and perfect his will really is.

9 Don't just pretend that you love others. Really love them. Hate what is wrong. Stand on the side of the good. 10 Love each other with genuine affection, and take delight in honoring each other. 11 Never be lazy in your work, but serve the Lord enthusiastically.

12 Be glad for all God is planning for you. Be patient in trouble, and always be prayerful. 13 When God's children are in need, be the one to

New International Version

16 Live in harmony with one another. Do not be proud, but be willing to associate with people of low position. Do not be conceited.

17 Do not repay anyone evil for evil. Be careful to do what is right in the eyes of everybody. 18 If it is possible, as far as it depends on you, live at peace with everyone. 19 Do not take revenge, my friends, but leave room for God's wrath, for it is written: "It is mine to avenge; I will repay," says the Lord. 20 On the contrary: "If your enemy is hungry, feed him; if he is thirsty, give him something to drink. In doing this, you will heap burning coals on his head." 21 Do not be overcome by evil, but overcome evil with good.

New Living Translation

help them out. And get into the habit of inviting guests home for dinner or, if they need lodging, for the night.

14 If people persecute you because you are a Christian, don't curse them; pray that God will bless them. 15 When others are happy, be happy with them. If they are sad, share their sorrow. 16 Live in harmony with each other. Don't try to act important, but enjoy the company of ordinary people. And don't think you know it all!

17 Never pay back evil for evil to anyone. Do things in such a way that everyone can see you are honorable. 18 Do your part to live in peace with everyone, as much as possible.

19 Dear friends, never avenge yourselves. Leave that to God. For it is written, "I will take vengeance; I will repay those who deserve it," says the Lord. 20 Instead, do what the Scriptures say: "If your enemies are hungry, feed them. If they are thirsty, give them something to drink, and they will be ashamed of what they have done to you."

21 Don't let evil get the best of you, but conquer evil by doing good.

GAINING BIBLICAL INSIGHT
Prayerfully dedicating my total being to Christ

*T*he word *dedicate* is used in many ways. We *dedicate* a phone line for Internet use. We *dedicate* books to honor people. We *dedicate* public buildings for specific purposes. However, the first definition of the word *dedicate* is "set apart for sacred use." In the Old Testament, vessels and instruments used for worship were not used in ordinary daily living. They were set apart for sacred use, "dedicated" in the truest sense.

When considering a woman's unlimited potential in Christ we must talk about her dedication. For some, a dedicated life suggests a monastic lifestyle, separate from ordinary interaction with people. In Romans 12, Paul talks about a dedicated manner of living in the everyday world.

The Reason for Dedication

Think of the things people dedicate their lives to such as sports, community service, or business achievements.

For what reasons might someone dedicate her life to one of these ends?

In verse 1, for what reason does Paul call Christians to a life of dedication?

The Demands of Dedication

PRESENT YOUR BODY

Paul's language reveals the intensity of his request. "I urge you," he says, to respond to God's marvelous love by presenting your body to Him. Paul's imploring words emphasize the high priority he places on dedication.

The word used for presentation of the body implies a completed act, something that is done once, and not a repetitive action such as offering the Old Testament sacrifices. To understand what Paul meant by "presenting" our bodies, we might compare this act to a soldier "presenting" himself for service to his country, or a slave "presenting" himself to his master. In these cases, the motivation might be duty or obligation. Paul appeals to the Romans to present themselves to God as an act of love.

Given the demands of the fast-paced world we live in, how do we offer our bodies as living sacrifices to the Lord in our daily lives?

RENEW YOUR MIND

The next dedication Paul calls for is the renewal of the mind (Romans 12:2). He mentions both positive and negative actions—what we are to do and what we are to avoid.

How is a believer to respond to the thought patterns of this world?

How are Christians to be transformed from secular thinking?

Note that Paul is appealing for the renewal of the mind, or the part of personality that relates to the world around us. It includes our mental capacity, our senses, and our emotions. He wants us to change our way of thinking which will affect the way we live.

What steps can we take regularly to renew our minds in Christ?

The Evidence of the Dedicated Life

Romans 12:9–21 includes a series of evidences of a dedicated life. In reading these statements, you can almost hear the compassion in Paul's tones as he writes to dear friends.

What characteristics mark the relationships among people who have sincere love for one another?

How does Paul tell us to relate to the following groups of people: the unkind, the celebrating, and the grieving?

Write a summary statement describing a dedicated Christian life from Paul's instructions to the Romans in this passage.

Paul encourages the Roman Christians to be "faithful in prayer." Consistency in prayer will be one mark of the dedicated Christian's life. The Book of Luke tells us about the prophetess, Anna, who dedicated her life totally to God. The demands on our lives may be much different than those on hers, but still we can learn from her what it means to have a dedicated life.

REFLECTING HIS IMAGE
Anna (Luke 2:36–38)

Life for me is coming to an end. I'm eighty-four years old and I've already outlived most of my friends and relatives. My own husband died more than sixty years ago. We had no children to care for, but we had seven wonderful years together.

A widow knows what it is to face a lonely and cheerless life, that's for sure. I never remarried, yet in place of what God took from me, He gave me more of himself! My culture doesn't allow a woman to pursue a career. So, I've had a lot of time on my hands.

I guess I could have spent my time reminiscing about the "good old days." Or I could have become the proverbial busybody, going from house to house spreading gossip and sticking my nose into other people's business. I suppose I could sit on the porch complaining to my neighbors about all my aches and pains, and the problems that come with growing older. But why?

Instead, I've tried to devote myself to loving God. I do love Him, you know. His house has become my house and spending time in His presence has been the joy of my life. I've spent many hours in the temple, night and day, fasting and praying.

One thing I know for certain after all these years is that God honors those who honor Him. He gave me the privilege of living to see what men of old died waiting for, the coming of the Messiah. And I can tell you it was worth the wait!

It happened like this. I was in the temple, where I always am, when His parents brought Him to offer Him to God as commanded in the Law. I made my way to my favorite corner spot and had just settled in when I looked up to see them. She cradled her son closely, protectively, very motherlike. Such a pretty young thing. *She looks small and vulnerable next to her tall husband,* I thought. I watched with curiosity as his arm rested slightly on her elbow, steering her to the center of the temple court where a line formed.

Hundreds of babies are presented in the temple every year, but suddenly my spirit confirmed it. This was the Child we had been waiting for. He was not just another pretty child. He was Jesus Christ, the promised Messiah! I had prayed, believed, and waited for this moment. It was time. The promise was fulfilled. Oh, what a glorious day it was! Coming up to them at the very moment of Simeon's blessing, I began at once to give thanks. And then, I told everybody who would listen about the goodness and greatness of our God.

I am old and frail, with lines from the seasons of life etched in my face. But no matter how old I may be, I don't ever have to retire from my walk with God. Yet, I somehow sense that I may very well be only weeks away from an event I've waited for all my life. I'm almost there, almost finished. I've lived and trusted and walked before God in faithfulness. I am fulfilled. Now, I can say with the Psalmist: "And I—in righteousness I will see your face; when I awake, I will be satisfied with seeing your likeness."[1]

EMBRACING THE PENTECOSTAL PERSPECTIVE

What is the Holy Spirit teaching me?

You have to admire that kind of dedication. Anna is an enigma to contemporary believers. What little we know of her life stands in stark contrast to how we live today. Tragic loss propelled her closer to her Heavenly

---

[1]Psalm 17:15.

Father. She chose to spend her life in His house. She was so keenly interested in looking for the Savior that she never missed a beat, even when He
showed up as an infant in the arms of His mother.

Dedication of this sort can't be manufactured; it is produced by the Holy
Spirit. And while the circumstances of your life and Anna's may differ, the
results need not. Asking Jesus to be the Lord of your life is just the first step
in a life of consecration. Then we must present our physical body for dedication and our mind for renewal. Every day the Holy Spirit guides us toward
those things that invite His presence and away from those that oppose God.

**Have you ever faced opposing choices, one that seemed justified
but dishonored God and one that defied logic but reflected God's
heart? What did you do?**

**How does the Spirit most often bring conviction (awareness of sin,
understanding truth, or a necessary action) to your attention?**

When are you most aware of the presence of God?

Dedication is not the result of a single act, but rather the accumulation
of many acts over a length of time. Most of us perform a good deed occasionally, simply by virtue of being in the right place at the right time.

However, the dedicated life requires an ongoing demonstration of Spirit-led living—love. Love is the mark of a dedicated disciple as listed by Paul in Romans 12:9–21.

How do you think Anna kept a tender heart before the Lord, avoiding a heart hardened in years of continuous service?

In what areas of your relationship with God do you need to be more dedicated?

One of the most remarkable things in Anna's story is her quick recognition of the Savior. It was more than being in the right place at the right time. Anna was introduced as a prophetess (Luke 2:36). God had positioned her to see His plan unfolding. He continues to do the same for every believer who is led by the Holy Spirit.

How have you seen evidence of God's working in an unexpected way?

Anna's response to seeing the Lord is one of immediate gratitude. It works the other way around, too. A grateful heart more readily sees God. **Share a testimony of thanks to God for something He has done this week.**

INVITING GOD TO CHANGE MY VIEW
What change is God asking me to make?

This lesson on dedication may have stirred feelings of inadequacy or guilt. Take a moment right now to discern the difference between true conviction and false condemnation. If anything is separating you and your Heavenly Father, now is the time to talk to Him about it. If you are allowing the enemy to induce condemnation, dismiss those thoughts. Instead, focus on God's goodness and His grace toward you, and seek His help to grow closer to Him.

Have you taken the first step in the life of dedication by asking Jesus to be your Lord? Does anything prevent you from experiencing the presence of God on a daily basis? Have you allowed difficulty to pull you away from a life of dedication? In what areas can you improve the demonstration of your dedication to the Lord?

Prayer
Father, I want to thank You for calling me to a life of dedication. I am so glad You are with me and my family in my home, at work, and at rest. I pray You will help me to be sensitive to the leading of the Spirit so my mind can continually be renewed. I do not want to be distanced from You by anything, especially that which would hinder me from total dedication to you. Let my life please You, Lord. I ask it in Jesus' name, Amen.

JOURNALING

Take a few moments to record your personal insights from the lesson.

Her Compelling Passion

CATCHING SIGHT
Introduction

MORE THAN THREE hundred years ago in Italy, three young men were pals. Antonio, nicknamed Tony, didn't share the talents of his two friends. When the three young men attended parties, his friends entertained with singing and playing musical instruments. Tony sat on the sidelines while others "stole the show."

Even though Tony couldn't sing or play a musical instrument, he wasn't completely without talents. He enjoyed whittling with his pocketknife. He knew a lot about wood and he had plenty of patience. He used that patience as a pupil of Niccolò Amati to learn to make a violin. He carefully selected the wood, sharpened his knife, and whittled away. He sandpapered, glued, and polished. Finally one day, Tony showed a beautiful violin to his friends.

Today if you ask any violinist whose violins are the best in the world, they will answer—Antonio Stradivari. The greatest desire in the hearts of many violinists is to play a Stradivarius violin. His violin-making technique has been imitated by many other artisans.

Suppose Tony had sulked in a corner because he had no special musical talent—he couldn't sing or play. The other two boys are forgotten, while the name of Antonio Stradivari is still remembered.

Jesus taught that some of us have one kind of talent, some have another kind, but whatever our talent may be, we should use it to the glory of God. If we ask God for help, He will reveal to us our special talents and help us develop them. Remember, it is not always those who are "the life of the party" who are most successful in life. Our problem is not that we are too passionate about bad things, but that we are not passionate enough about good things.

Discover your gifts and become passionate about using them for the Lord.

GETTING FOCUSED

Begin your study by sharing thoughts on the following:

What you love to do when no one's looking really defines what you are passionate about. You are created to make a difference! What do you love to do that could be used in the kingdom of God? What is holding you back from using your gifts now?

Bible Reading

Romans 12:3–8

New International Version	*New Living Translation*

3 For by the grace given me I say to every one of you: Do not think of yourself more highly than you ought, but rather think of yourself with sober judgment, in accordance with the measure of faith God has given you. 4 Just as each of us has one body with many members, and these members do not all have the same function, 5 so in Christ we who are many form one body, and each member belongs to all the others. 6 We have different gifts, according to the grace given us. If a man's gift is prophesying, let him use it in proportion to his faith. 7 If it is serving, let him serve; if it is teaching, let him teach; 8 if it is encouraging, let him encourage; if it is contributing to the needs of others, let him give generously; if it is leadership, let him govern diligently; if it is showing mercy, let him do it cheerfully.

3 As God's messenger, I give each of you this warning: Be honest in your estimate of yourselves, measuring your value by how much faith God has given you. 4 Just as our bodies have many parts and each part has a special function, 5 so it is with Christ's body. We are all parts of his one body, and each of us has different work to do. And since we are all one body in Christ, we belong to each other, and each of us needs all the others.

6 God has given each of us the ability to do certain things well. So if God has given you the ability to prophesy, speak out when you have faith that God is speaking through you. 7 If your gift is that of serving others, serve them well. If you are a teacher, do a good job of teaching. 8 If your gift is to encourage others, do it! If you have money, share it generously. If God has given you

New Living Translation
leadership ability, take the responsibility seriously. And if you have a gift for showing kindness to others, do it gladly.

GAINING BIBLICAL INSIGHT
Discovering and using my unique gifts

The word *passion* like *dedication* is used in many ways. Derived from the Latin word for suffering, *passion* is frequently used of Christ's sufferings. We commonly use the word to describe our most compelling feelings. We can have a *passion* for chocolate or a *passion* to change the world, using the same word but with vastly different implications.

What do we mean when we talk about the compelling passion of a person's life?

As we walk with the Lord, we become passionate about what He cares about: His Word and His work. Understanding the gifts of grace in Romans 12:3–8 will help us find our place of ministry and compelling passion.

A Right Understanding of Ourselves

Before Paul describes the gifts of grace, he deals with the mental attitude of those who use them.

What is the appropriate mindset of the person who will use a gift of grace (verse 3)?

Having a proper evaluation of oneself may be the most difficult mental exercise. Paul warns against regarding oneself too highly, challenging us to remember any ministry we have is because of God's work through us.

Sometimes we go in the other direction and we put ourselves down, underestimating what God could do through us. The appeal here is to see ourselves in the right perspective, redeemed by God with great potential.

A Right Understanding of Our Relationships in the Body

Paul moves quickly to relationships in the Church, using the human body as a metaphor. Right thinking about ourselves prepares us for right thinking about others.

What comparisons does Paul make between the human body and the Church as the body of Christ (verses 4,5)?

The metaphor illustrates the unity and diversity of the Church. As individuals we are vastly different, but we function in compatible relationship. We appreciate our differences without being competitive. We do not need to envy another's gifts, or exalt our own. We suffer and rejoice with others because we are members of the same Body.

A Right Understanding of the Gifts of Grace

Paul explains the gifts are given because of God's grace, not our own merit. The ministry gifts within the Church are evidence of God's presence among us. Let us look at the gifts individually and their relationship to each other.

Prophecy. A prophet is one who proclaims truth, not with a new revelation but in a new understanding of truth. The prophet speaks the Word of God to the hearts of people in the power of the Holy Spirit.

Serving. The servant ministers to material needs of fellow believers and others outside the Church. The word for *serving* is used in Acts 6 when the disciples daily served the widows.

Teaching. A teacher wants believers to have a clear understanding of Scripture, addressing the mind as a prophet addresses the heart. Priscilla and Aquila modeled this gift when they instructed Apollos in the way of the Lord.

Encouraging. The encourager comes along beside believers to keep them walking with the Lord. As a prophet and teacher speaks to the heart and mind, the encourager addresses the will.

Contributing. The contributor is concerned with physical needs, providing goods which the servant may distribute. Contributors are urged to give without any private agenda or motivation.

Leadership. In any group of two or more people, one will emerge as the leader. Consequently, diligent leadership is needed in many areas of the Church's ministry.

Showing Mercy. Occasions will arise when the Church must reach out in mercy to people in need which should be done with a joyful heart, not from duty or necessity. People needing mercy need to absorb your joyful spirit as much as they need your act of mercy.

An Illustration of the Gifts of Grace

To observe the gifts of grace functioning, imagine a crowd has gathered in your church's fellowship hall for a dinner. Suddenly, the legs on one of the food-covered tables fold under, dumping all the tasty dishes of food on the floor. The gifts of grace begin to function.

Who runs quickly to the kitchen to gather towels, mops, and a trash can?

Who assigns someone to use the mops and towels, gets someone to reset the table, and assures the hungry crowd that food will soon be available?

Who puts an arm around the kitchen workers to assure them everything will work out so they will not give up?

Who whips out the checkbook to send someone to the nearest fast-food restaurant for replacement food?

Who finds the embarrassed person who set the table up in the first place and says "Any one of us could have made the same mistake"?

Who explains that the problem was the clamp holding the leg had not been firmly in place, with the injunction to be sure the clamp is secure the next time?

Who sees this accident as the perfect illustration of how disaster follows when someone does not heed God's Word to "stand firm" in the faith?

The leader, the servant, and the contributor address immediate needs. The encourager and the one showing mercy address personal needs, while the prophet and teacher are concerned with long-range needs. All ministries are needed to keep the Church functioning.

The hungry world is waiting to be fed the Word of God. The Church must be about the business of providing for them.

The persons who surrounded Jesus in His ministry here on earth had very different gifts. One whose compelling passion was showing mercy was Mary of Bethany. Let's look in on her as she shows her gift of grace at work.

REFLECTING HIS IMAGE
Mary of Bethany (John 12:1–8)

The narrow, stony path seemed longer than she remembered. Was it a week since her last visit to the spot? Lately, hours and days and weeks ran together, making her thoughts a cloudy haze of confusion. But then, organization had never been her strength. *Let Martha worry about household chores and schedules and propriety,* she thought as she hurried along. *My mission this morning is important whether or not anyone else understands. More than important. Urgent!*

The soil was still damp from the morning dew, making the spot easy to see. Kneeling at the foot of the massive sycamore tree, she glanced right and then left. *No one in sight.* Within seconds, Mary lifted the treasure from the shallow hole in the ground. She brushed the red clay away from the edges of the delicate jar, opened the lid, and carefully studied its contents. *A denarius-a-day wage—three hundred denarii to cover a man's wages for almost a year. Enough to buy the perfume.* Clutching the jar tightly for courage and reassurance, her thoughts raced ahead. *Jesus is in town, a guest of Simon. Tonight I will demonstrate how grateful I am for my Lord's faithfulness to me. I'm sure. More than sure. Certain!*

The knock on the door could not have come at a more inconvenient time. Another knock— harder, louder. Leaving his position at the table, Judas wiped his hands and opened the door. Mary stood in the doorway. The room grew quiet. Silent love can be a mighty force, an ally. Mary was intent as she made her way past Simon, Judas, and the others. Her eyes surveyed the room until at last she saw Him, reclining at the table. Love, mingled with passion and purpose, drove her to the other end of the room until at last she found herself kneeling at the feet of Jesus. Smiling, she looked into His eyes, remembering other times like this—times when she sat at Jesus' feet to learn, to praise, to grow. The glory of His presence completely filled her mind as she savored the sweetness of this moment.

In one graceful movement, Mary lifted the treasure from beneath her tunic, oblivious to the others around her. Opening the bottle, she poured the costly perfume on the Lord's feet and began to wipe them dry with her hair.

"What are you doing?" someone gasped.

Judas shouted, "Why wasn't this oil sold and the money given to the poor? It would have easily brought three hundred silver pieces."[1]

Some of the guests swelled up in anger, nearly bursting with indignation. Undaunted by their protests, Mary continued to pour her praise on the feet of Jesus. *Grateful,* she thought as she wept quietly. *No, more than grateful. Honored!*

"Jesus said, 'Let her alone. She's anticipating and honoring the day of my burial. You always have the poor with you. You don't always have me.'"[2]

Silent moments later, Mary stood to her feet. Slowly, awkwardly, she backed away from the table. But *her* eyes never left *His* eyes. She knew positively that Jesus understood her and loved her for who she was. *To some I seem radical and foolish and wasteful* she thought. *But I stand accepted. More than accepted. Unashamed!*

---

[1]John 12:5, *The Message.*
[2]John 12:8, *The Message.*

EMBRACING THE PENTECOSTAL PERSPECTIVE

What is the Holy Spirit teaching me?

Mary's tribute to her Lord presents a beautiful picture of Spirit-birthed passion. It is the kind of passion with a singular focus—Jesus Christ, and boundless application—every person who knows Him or needs to know Him. This passion does not require volume for expression; it is not obnoxious. Rather, compelling passion enables the person in whom the Spirit stirs to live and serve with amazing strength. We give what we have because we are compelled by love.

The love of the Lord is unlike anything we've ever experienced. Mary's passion was a response to that love and the acceptance she received. She was freed from the worry of what others thought of her, because it simply didn't matter when she knew Jesus loved her. Likewise, we are free to use our gifts of grace to build up the body of Christ, because we want to please Jesus.

How do you express your love for the Lord?

Do you compare your expressions of worship and gifts of grace to others and feel inadequate at times? Is this healthy or unhealthy?

Have you ever been surprised by the depth of your love for the Lord? Describe the experience that brought about such awareness.

This passion compelled Mary to go somewhere and do something that defies the average person's understanding. She didn't walk into an intimidating setting and give something of enormous value having been motivated by an adolescent crush or an attempt to buy affection. For these she would have still drawn ridicule but accomplished nothing further. Instead, she risked the contempt of others to perform an extraordinary display of love.

Has your love for the Lord ever propelled you into a place of service, a conversation, or some other act that was considerably outside your comfort zone? Explain.

Describe a time when you gave sacrificially out of love for another.

Mary's passion secured her a place in church history for which Jesus prophesied she would always be remembered. Of course, Mary was not seeking lasting fame, and she probably did not understand the prophetic significance of her action. Sometimes participation in the prophetic purposes of the Lord is not a matter of foresight, so much as it is proclamation.

How, specifically, are you using your gifts of grace to proclaim God's love for the world?

How do you want to serve others?

INVITING GOD TO CHANGE MY VIEW
What change is God asking me to make?

Spirit-birthed passion differs from the world's idea of passion in both its intensity and its application. Loving the Lord and acting out of that love is not momentary or incidental. If properly nurtured, it should grow in strength throughout one's relationship with the Lord. Remember, God creates a new heart in us at the new birth. Passion is not a matter of personality.

Every person can experience compelling passion.

Is your love for the Lord something that you know, feel, or are moved by? Would you like it to be all three? Do you know what your unique gifts of grace are? Have you hardened your heart to the Lord through distance or disobedience? Will you invite the Holy Spirit to tenderize your heart toward the Lord, igniting a consuming passion within? Do you need to ask Jesus to give you a new heart and life, one in which He is Lord?

Prayer

Lord Jesus, I love You. I know I sometimes say it without really thinking about it, but I want You to know that I mean it. I also know that I have a long way to grow in my love for You. I want my love for You to be so fresh, so full, and so compelling that I am moved beyond my own fears and weaknesses to use my gifts for you. Let me be an illustration of Your love, Lord. Communicate through me with clarity and power. Help me to become more expressive in using my gifts and less reserved, because I have no reservations about Your love for me. In Your name, Amen.

JOURNALING

Take a few moments to record your personal insights from the lesson.

Her Life's Mission

CATCHING SIGHT

Introduction

A GREAT ARTIST completed a painting he titled "Jesus and the Children." The picture portrayed the loving Savior. Sitting all about Him were little children; one sat on His knee. The Master's face was smiling, and the children knew He was their Friend.

But one thing was wrong with the picture—all the children were white. Some Christians called the artist's attention to this fault in the painting. He set about at once correcting it. Patiently and carefully he transformed the children around Jesus into boys and girls from all races—black, yellow, red, white, and brown. With this correction the picture became famous and loved by Christians everywhere.

Like that artist, it is easy to have tunnel vision and see only what directly touches your life situation. However, if you are determined to make a difference, Jesus will take your life and weave it with others who have the same goal, to develop a church that makes a difference. Then Jesus can weave your church with other churches that have the same mission to touch their world. Surrendering to Jesus is the first step in aligning our individual lives with God's mission for the Church.

GETTING FOCUSED

Begin your study by considering the following:

The mission of the Church is the responsibility of every member of the body of Christ. This is not the time to sit back and watch others perform. We are all called to fulfill the Great Commission. What keeps people from answering God's call in the Great Commission?

Bible Reading

Psalm 40:5; Jeremiah 29:11; Matthew 16:18; Matthew 28:19; Acts 1:8

New International Version	*New Living Translation*
Psalm 40:5 Many, O Lord my God, are the wonders you have done. The things you planned for us no one can recount to you; were I to speak and tell of them, they would be too many to declare.	Psalm 40:5 O Lord my God, you have done many miracles for us. Your plans for us are too numerous to list. If I tried to recite all your wonderful deeds, I would never come to the end of them.
Jeremiah 29:11 "For I know the plans I have for you," declares the Lord, "plans to prosper you and not to harm you, plans to give you hope and a future."	Jeremiah 29:11 "For I know the plans I have for you," says the Lord. "They are plans for good and not for disaster, to give you a future and a hope."
Matthew 16:18 "And I tell you that you are Peter, and on this rock I will build my church, and the gates of Hades will not overcome it."	Matthew 16:18 "Now I say to you that you are Peter, and upon this rock I will build my church, and all the powers of hell will not conquer it."
Matthew 28:19 "Therefore go and make disciples of all nations, baptizing them in the name of the Father and of the Son and of the Holy Spirit."	Matthew 28:19 Therefore, go and make disciples of all the nations, baptizing them in the name of the Father and the Son and the Holy Spirit.
Acts 1:8 "But you will receive power when the Holy Spirit comes	Acts 1:8 "But when the Holy Spirit has come upon you, you will

New International Version	*New Living Translation*
on you; and you will be my wit-nesses in Jerusalem, and in all Judea and Samaria, and to the ends of the earth."	receive power and will tell people about me everywhere—in Jerusalem, throughout Judea, in Samaria, and to the ends of the earth."

GAINING BIBLICAL INSIGHT
Aligning my life with God's mission for the world

When reading the Psalms, you sometimes feel as if you are on the Judean hills with the Psalmist overlooking the pastoral landscape and surveying the star-studded heavens. As you stand there, the Psalmist lifts your vision beyond the horizon to consider the God who created this beauty. He comments that nature reveals the creative power and majesty of the God who is a God of design with plans for His people. We know from Scripture that God's ultimate mission for the world is to reconcile mankind to himself, restoring the relationship lost in Eden.

God as a God of Design

Read Psalm 40:5. **What are some of the many wonders of God the Psalmist might have been thinking about as he penned these words?**

What do you think is some of the most convincing evidence in nature that God is a God of design?

From the foundation of the earth, God planned to redeem lost humanity. This planning is also one of His wonders.

God's Plan for a Nation

In the Old Testament, we see God's unfolding plan by the establishment of a nation through which He could reveal His love for mankind. He called Abraham to leave the idol-worshipping nation where he had been raised. God made a covenant with Abraham that through his family, all nations would be blessed. The twelve children of Abraham's grandson Jacob became founders of the nation of Israel.

As we continue reading, we see the rise and fall of Israel as its people failed to follow God. Finally, they were taken into captivity because of their sins. At this low point in their history, God spoke to the prophet Jeremiah that He still had plans for this nation.

According to Jeremiah 29:11, what are the components of God's plan for Israel?

What does this prophecy by Jeremiah reveal to us about God's nature?

From our perspective, we see a nation whom we assume God would abandon. God remained true to His own purpose. He is a God of compassion, so He continued pursuing His plan for His people. No wonder Jeremiah was inspired to write, "O great and powerful God, whose name is the Lord Almighty, great are your purposes and mighty are your deeds. Your eyes are open to all the ways of men" (Jeremiah 32:18,19).

God's Plan for the Church

In the New Testament, we see God's continued plan for reconciling mankind to himself. Jesus came in human form to reveal God the Father, including His wonderful plan for our salvation. He told of God's continuing plan for building relationships with people through a new entity called the Church (Matthew 16:18). Jesus briefly referred to the Church one day while talking to His disciples, but His instructions to them before His Ascension laid the groundwork on which the Church was built.

We call the last words of Jesus before His Ascension the Great Commission (Matthew 28:19,20). This is Jesus' instructions to the disciples to teach all nations what they had learned from Him—that God is a God of love who wants to draw all people into a personal relationship with himself.

How is the Church today fulfilling the Great Commission given by Jesus?

Acts 1:8 records a promise Jesus gave the disciples. They would not have to fulfill the Great Commission in their own strength. The Holy Spirit would be sent to help them.

When the disciples followed Jesus' instructions, they received the empowerment of the Spirit and the Church was born. As you trace the history of the Church, you see it grew exactly as Jesus said: Jerusalem first, then Judea and Samaria, and finally to all of the then-known world. Since that time, successive generations of believers have carried the gospel throughout the earth.

God's Plan for Me Personally

God is still at work in the world, carrying out His mission of reconciling people to himself. When we look at our world, we need to look beyond the socio-political scene to see how God is at work. Wherever the gospel is preached in the power of the Spirit, believers come together and the Church continues to grow.

The Church can fulfill the Great Commission only as individuals become involved. The questions we must ask ourselves are:

What am I doing personally to fulfill the Great Commission?

Have I aligned my life with God's mission for the world?

Have I received the Holy Spirit to help me fulfill my mission?

Let's look at one woman Deborah who fit uniquely into the plan of God. She is an example of a woman who understood her mission and fulfilled it in the difficult times. Her roles of prophet and military leader were unusual, yet she had a vital part in the history of Israel. Like Deborah, we can respond to the call of God to be involved with what God is doing in our times.

REFLECTING HIS IMAGE
Deborah (Judges 4 and 5)

Barak was not surprised when a messenger brought word from Deborah to come quickly. As commander of Israel's army, he knew what that meant. Deborah received direct orders from God. And in matters of national security and warfare, high-ranking officials depended on her wise counsel.

A warm breeze blew in the morning air as Deborah rested beneath the palm tree. Looking across the distance to the faces of the people approaching, she breathed deeply and whispered, "I trust You, God." A long line formed, snaking across the desert. Men and women throughout the region came for answers, justice, and wisdom. As God's prophet, Deborah spent most of her time meeting those needs. Faith speaks boldly. Unlike many of her friends, she had ample faith.

"This way," the messenger said as he directed Barak to the front of the line. Barak followed the servant obediently, expectantly. Court was in session. Deborah, the only female judge of the twelve who guided Israel, was about to speak. She said to him, "It has become clear that God, the God of Israel, commands you: Go to Mount Tabor and prepare for battle. Take ten companies of soldiers from Naphtali and Zebulun. I'll take care of getting Sisera, the leader of Jabin's army, to the Kishon River with all his chariots and troops. And I'll make sure you win the battle."[1]

Barak said, "If you go with me, I'll go. But if you don't go with me, I won't go."[2]

Deborah answered without hesitation. "Of course I'll go with you. But understand that with an attitude like that, there'll be no glory in it for you. God will use a woman's hand to take care of Sisera."[3]

---

[1]Judges 4:6,7, *The Message.*
[2]Judges 4:8, *The Message.*
[3]Judges 4:9, *The Message.*

It didn't take her long to pack her things and accompany the army into battle. Twenty years of Canaanite oppression were at last coming to an end. Deborah paused, considering the coming battle. *The Israelites cried to the Lord for help. He is about to deliver us. I do not doubt the outcome, Lord. You have spoken. We are merely to obey.*

Later, she knew just the right time to command Barak, "Attack! This is the day the Lord will hand Sisera over to you."[4] But Barak would not get the glory for winning the battle. It happened just as Deborah said. A woman, Jael, killed the mighty Sisera.

After their stunning victory, Deborah cried aloud, "Villages in Israel were deserted . . . until I, Deborah, took a stand . . . as a mother of Israel."[5] Her courageous mission was not impossible. God spoke and she obeyed.

The next day found her writing a song with Barak, a melody of praise to God for His deliverance of Israel. Standing in the shade of the Palm of Deborah, the prophet and judge tilted back her head, lifted her eyes to God, and softly hummed the song of victory that future generations would rejoice to hear—God delivers His people!

EMBRACING THE PENTECOSTAL PERSPECTIVE
What is the Holy Spirit teaching me?

Aren't you glad you're on the Lord's side? Sometimes we say that as a cliché, but put aside for a minute the trite phrases about victory and the sometimes thoughtlessly sung choruses about stomping on the enemy. Then separate yourself from the commonness with which you occasionally might treat your relationship to God, and examine how your life is aligning with God's mission for the world.

First, savor with renewed awe the miracle of your salvation. Can you believe Creator God chooses *you?* He loves *you.* He sent Jesus to pay the price for *your* sins. And, that's not all. He wants each and every one of us to have a personal relationship with Him.

If that thought makes you uncomfortable, it is probably due to one or two reasons: you haven't yet accepted the invitation to join God and/or you aren't living your life in such a way that reflects your decision for those around you to see. In either case, it is time to embrace the truths that enabled Deborah to fulfill her life's mission.

Deborah didn't spend her days listening to people's problems because she

---

[4] *Voices of Faith*, 282.
[5] Ibid., 283.

thought it was fun. Nor did she ride off to war because life under the palm tree was getting a little dull. Rather, she did both of these things because she understood the heart of God for people. God wants people to be saved from the oppression of the enemy and live a renewed life, both of which are possible only through Jesus Christ.

Do you think about the lostness of humanity on a regular basis? Why or why not?

How do you keep a tender heart toward those who need to meet Jesus?

Why do some believers treat witnessing as optional or someone else's responsibility?

What are you doing to reach people for the Lord?

When a car hits an object or a particularly deep pothole, the alignment of the vehicle may become skewed. Without repair, the car tends to pull to one side or the other instead of traveling straight ahead. People are like cars. Any little bump in the road has the potential to send us in a direction we shouldn't go—unless we're aligned with the Lord. None of us would have blamed Deborah if she had ridiculed Barak for his lack of courage or refused to accompany him. Instead, because she had aligned herself with God's salvation mission, she also aligned herself with God's people to accomplish that mission.

How does the Holy Spirit serve as an early warning light, indicating when we have an alignment problem?

What in your life is pulling you away from fully participating in God's salvation mission?

God's mission offers a variety of roles: battle leader (Barak); teacher, encourager, supporter, conversation initiator (Deborah); willing helper (Jael) to name just a few. **Tell which role(s) you are most comfortable with and how you fulfill that role in your life.**

INVITING GOD TO CHANGE MY VIEW
What change is God asking me to make?

Deborah's story communicates many truths, but perhaps none so clearly as the fact that nothing is impossible with God. God doesn't view twenty years of oppression as a problem. He uses a woman in leadership to take care of a problem with a unique solution.

One of the easiest ways to align ourselves with God's mission is to identify with these exhilarating possibilities. God saves, delivers, has a place for you, and can use you to help reach the world—if you will invite Him to do so! Whatever bumps in the road have sent you in the wrong direction, the repair can start now.

The biggest alignment issue is that of your heart. Have you given it to Jesus? It is as simple as admitting you have sinned, asking Jesus to forgive your sins, and inviting Him to be your Lord.

Perhaps there are other areas of alignment in your life that require fine-tuning. Do you need God to cultivate in you a heart for the lost? Do you desire more courage to witness? Have you been baptized in the Holy Spirit? Do you need God to clarify your place in His great mission?

Prayer
Father God, thank You so much for Your great love. It is simply astounding that You love people—all people—so much! I want to reflect Your heart, Father. Fill me with Your Holy Spirit and give me a boldness to talk to others

about Your Son. Forgive me for making excuses. Use me, like You did Deborah and countless others, to fulfill Your miraculous mission. I trust You, Lord, to enable me to do anything You call me to do. In Jesus' name, Amen.

JOURNALING

Take a few moments to record your personal insights from the lesson.

Her Servant's Heart

LESSON SEVEN

CATCHING SIGHT
Introduction

*A*N UNEXPECTED POWER outage plunged the house into darkness. A brief search turned up a flashlight, but it hadn't been used in over a year. When Sarah flipped the switch nothing happened; the flashlight gave no light. Sarah unscrewed the top and shook the flashlight to get the batteries out, but they wouldn't budge. Finally, after some effort, they came loose. What a mess! Battery acid had corroded the entire inside of the flashlight. The batteries were new when Sarah had put them in, and she had stored the flashlight in a safe, warm place. But there was one problem. Those batteries weren't made to be warm and comfortable. They were designed for usefulness—to provide light.

It's the same for Christians. We weren't created to be warm, safe, and comfortable. You and I were made for usefulness—to put our love to work; to apply our patience in difficult, trying situations; to let our light shine as servants in His Kingdom.

Obviously, most people would not consider the title *servant* a glamorous one. It is not one that most would list on their resumés. However, knowledge apart from application falls short of God's desire for His children. He wants us to apply what we learn so that we will change, grow, and be tools that He can use to touch others.

GETTING FOCUSED

Begin your study by sharing thoughts on the following:

More than ever, selfishness has become a way of life. Too many people believe the word *servant* means "serve me." What do you think of when you hear the word *servant*?

Bible Reading

Philippians 2:1–13

New International Version

1 If you have any encouragement from being united with Christ, if any comfort from his love, if any fellowship with the Spirit, if any tenderness and compassion, 2 then make my joy complete by being like-minded, having the same love, being one in spirit and purpose.
3 Do nothing out of selfish ambition or vain conceit, but in humility consider others better than yourselves.
4 Each of you should look not only to your own interests, but also to the interests of others.

5 Your attitude should be the same as that of Christ Jesus:
6 Who, being in very nature God, did not consider equality with God something to be grasped, 7 but made himself nothing, taking the very nature of a servant, being made in human likeness. 8 And being found in appearance as a man, he humbled himself and became obedient to death—even death on a cross! 9 Therefore God exalted him to the highest place

New Living Translation

1 Is there any encouragement from belonging to Christ? Any comfort from his love? Any fellowship together in the Spirit? Are your hearts tender and sympathetic?
2 Then make me truly happy by agreeing wholeheartedly with each other, loving one another, and working together with one heart and purpose.

3 Don't be selfish; don't live to make a good impression on others. Be humble, thinking of others as better than yourself. 4 Don't think only about your own affairs, but be interested in others, too, and what they are doing.

5 Your attitude should be the same that Christ Jesus had.
6 Though he was God, he did not demand and cling to his rights as God. 7 He made himself nothing; he took the humble position of a slave and appeared in human form. 8 And in human form he obediently humbled himself even further by dying a criminal's death on a

New International Version

and gave him the name that is above every name, 10 that at the name of Jesus every knee should bow, in heaven and on earth and under the earth, 11 and every tongue confess that Jesus Christ is Lord, to the glory of God the Father.

12 Therefore, my dear friends, as you have always obeyed—not only in my presence, but now much more in my absence—continue to work out your salvation with fear and trembling, 13 for it is God who works in you to will and to act according to his good purpose.

New Living Translation

cross. 9 Because of this, God raised him up to the heights of heaven and gave him a name that is above every other name, 10 so that at the name of Jesus every knee will bow, in heaven and on earth and under the earth, 11 and every tongue will confess that Jesus Christ is Lord, to the glory of God the Father.

12 Dearest friends, you were always so careful to follow my instructions when I was with you. And now that I am away you must be even more careful to put into action God's saving work in your lives, obeying God with deep reverence and fear. 13 For God is working in you, giving you the desire to obey him and the power to do what pleases him.

GAINING BIBLICAL INSIGHT
Maintaining a servant's heart in all I do

*I*n this high-tech age very few of us have servants in our homes. Food can be prepared quickly with electronic appliances and microwave ovens, making kitchen help unnecessary. We buy automatic washers and dryers instead of hiring laundry workers. Cell phones and instant-messaging computers replace messengers in our fast-paced society. Although advanced technology may perform many functions of servants, it can never take the place of a servant's heart. That kind of heart is found only in people.

God gifts individuals for service in a variety of ways. Although our gifts may differ, we all have one thing in common—the need to maintain a servant's heart in all we do, following the example of servanthood modeled by Jesus.

Jesus' Teaching and Example of Servanthood

From the earliest days of following Jesus, the disciples were convinced He was the Messiah. They thought He would set up a kingdom and release Israel from Roman rule. Even when He spoke plainly of His coming death and resurrection, they did not understand what He was saying because of their preconceived ideas. Instead, they argued over who would be the greatest in the coming Kingdom. At that point, Jesus became explicit about the difference between His Kingdom and others.

Read Matthew 20:20–28. **What comparisons did Jesus make between His leadership style and that of Gentile rulers?**

A few days later, Jesus gave His disciples an example of servanthood when He surprised them at their last meal together before His Crucifixion by rising from the table and washing their feet. "I have set you an example that you should do as I have done for you," He said (John 13:15). They had been disputing again as to who would be the greatest in the Kingdom. "I am among you as one who serves," He reminded them again (Luke 22:27).

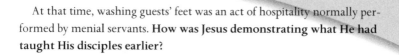

At that time, washing guests' feet was an act of hospitality normally per-formed by menial servants. **How was Jesus demonstrating what He had taught His disciples earlier?**

In what ways does this example of servanthood translate into today's culture?

Jesus' Attitude as a Servant

Paul taught the Philippians they should have the attitude of Christ in their relationships with one another. Read Philippians 2:3–8 to see Paul's description of the attitude of Christ.

What qualities of Christ's nature referred to in this passage should be found in His followers?

What is the correlation between humility and obedience?

How does a servant's role illustrate both humility and obedience?

How do Christians manifest these qualities in their lives?

A Lifestyle of Servanthood

Paul began this chapter in Philippians with a plea for unity among the believers. He was writing from prison to a group of Christians who were facing persecution, pleading with them to maintain unity as a means of spiritual strength.

What blessings are listed in verse 1 that Christians experience by being united with Christ?

In what ways will these blessings be maintained in the Christian community, according to verse 2?

What attitudes should be avoided so that unity can be maintained (verse 3)?

Paul greatly desired for the believers to experience unity with each other just as they had experienced unity with Christ. This unity would be possible as they humbly considered the interests of others as much as their own. They would think like Christ, not that they would all have the same opinions but the same mind-set. They would love like Christ and have the humble, yet confident, spirit of Christ.

Paul concludes the description of the obedient servitude of Christ by looking to the future time of His exaltation when all creation acknowledges Him as Lord (Philippians 2:9–11). Those who walk with Christ now as humble, obedient servants will rejoice with Him when He comes into His Kingdom as King of kings and Lord of lords.

Martha of Bethany is another scriptural example of a person who learned to have a servant's heart. At first she served with the wrong attitude, but later we see her serving in true humility. Let's hear her story.

REFLECTING HIS IMAGE
Martha (Luke 10:41,42; John 12:2)

I've always loved company. I grew up in a spacious home where the door was seldom closed to outsiders. A constant stream of relatives and friends graced our table with their presence and conversation.

Now, I especially love having Jesus in our home, and His disciples are always welcome. Their visits to Bethany are one of the true joys of my life. Lazarus says they will be here in less than two hours. Where has the day gone? There is water to be drawn from the well, more food to prepare, and a table to set. Where is Mary when I need her?

No matter. It doesn't upset me like it did last time. Jesus told me that day that I had become too consumed and worried about "doing" and not enough about "being." I was scurrying around the house that day, as only I can, wanting everyone to do their best for Him, including my sister who sat before the Master hanging on every word He said. I was pulled away by all I had to do in the kitchen. So, later I interrupted Him.

" 'Master, don't you care that my sister has abandoned the kitchen to me? Tell her to lend me a hand.' The Master said, 'Martha, dear Martha, you're fussing far too much and getting yourself worked up over nothing. One thing only is essential, and Mary has chosen it—it's the main course, and won't be taken from her.' "[1]

His soft rebuke came as a surprise, and at the time, His words cut right through me. But I am learning that I too can have a deeper relationship with Him. And I am working hard to change my thinking.

The day my brother Lazarus died was the saddest day of my life. After all, he is more than a brother to me. He's my confidant, my provider, and my friend. Losing him was devastating. Burying him was surreal.

I remember the precise moment four days after his death when I heard that Jesus was on His way to our house. This time, I dropped everything and

---

[1]Luke 10:40–42, *The Message.*

went out to meet Him. *The mourners can care for themselves. Mary, stay inside if you must. But I need Jesus to console me.* The fact is, if Jesus had been there, Lazarus wouldn't have died. And I told Him so. Jesus understood that my remark wasn't a rebuke. He said, "I am the resurrection and the life."[2] And I believe Him! He is the Son of God! He raised my brother from the dead. It wasn't the far-off event I thought it would be. It happened right before my eyes! That physical miracle resulted in a spiritual miracle in me.

I now understand that Jesus doesn't want me to stop being me. He loves me and appreciates my warm hospitality. But He also wants me to know and remember, beyond a doubt, *who* I serve and *why*. Once an annoyance, I now create a "to do" list each morning that begins with asking God to give me the true heart of a servant and to lead me to the people He wants me to serve. I have learned that my attitude about serving means everything.

Tonight, I will offer Jesus my best. The food I serve at my table will be wonderfully presented. My house will be clean and comfortable. But I will not be distracted with home care and obligations. I will simply serve my guests, conscious that both serving and learning are duties, and in both I should honor God.

EMBRACING THE PENTECOSTAL PERSPECTIVE
What is the Holy Spirit teaching me?

Martha's story requires little interpretation. Most women do not have difficulty relating to her struggle; we all juggle too-busy lives. At the most basic level, Martha's problem was one of attitude and priorities. Even some mature believers find it challenging to keep first things first. Thankfully, Jesus sent the Holy Spirit to walk alongside us and point to the Savior. By fine-tuning several areas of our lives, the Spirit enables us to focus on the Lord and serve Him.

Do you struggle to keep your priorities straight? If so, why?

---

[2]John 11:25.

Where should your relationship with the Lord be on the priority list? Does your schedule currently reflect this?

What helps you to reprioritize and/or successfully live according to correct priorities?

If we fail to yield to the Spirit's leading about priorities in our lives, then serving will suffer one of two serious setbacks. It will either never happen or it will become an act of drudgery that takes the life out of us, instead of adding life to the kingdom of God. Neither option is God's will. Martha teaches us that serving is energizing and enjoyable when we use our gifts and talents in humility and with a Christlike attitude. This means considering others more than ourselves.

Identify one of your gifts or talents. (Everything from good listener to best brownie maker counts here!)

Share the gifts or talents you see in others you are acquainted with that they may not see in themselves.

How do you avoid burnout and keep from becoming "weary in well-doing?"

Are you making excuses for not serving? Are the reasons legitimate or contrived?

When is it okay not to serve?

Ultimately, serving is an others-focused attitude. Paul said it best: "For we do not preach ourselves, but Jesus Christ as Lord, and ourselves as your servants for Jesus' sake" (2 Corinthians 4:5). Sometimes this kind of service taps our God-given abilities, while other times it simply challenges the status of our hearts. In the latter case, we are called upon to do something that doesn't necessarily fit our passion, but we participate anyway because our hearts are submissive to the Spirit's leading, and we are focused on the needs of others.

Describe the ideal attitude a believer should have when serving. Do you have it?

When people or circumstances are difficult, how do you keep a servant's heart?

Share an experience that relates one of the blessings of serving.

INVITING GOD TO CHANGE MY VIEW

What change is God asking me to make?

One of the great things about serving is that it is not just an opportunity for us to share the wealth of our talents, time, or efforts with others. Serving is always a prime learning laboratory as well. It provides a wonderful way for us to be reminded of our dependence on God, and to learn that in our weakness, He is always strong. Serving leads to transformation.

Transformation begins with a life devoted to the Lord. Today, if anything separates you from the Lord, now is the time to close the distance. Would you like to invite Jesus to forgive your sins and be your Savior?

What do you need to be a better servant for the Lord: a good attitude, more understanding of your spiritual gifts, boldness to get involved? Do you need discipline to get your time and priorities in order? Do you need the Lord to do a work of renewal in your life to bring fresh vision and strength for your service?

Prayer

Lord, I want to thank You for allowing me to serve You. It is more than a privilege; it is a source of constant joy! Working with You and for You is the highest calling. Though it sometimes takes a lower form, please help me to always see my service as an act of worship and obedience to You. Help me listen to the voice of Your Spirit and heed His directions. Stop me in my tracks if I stray from Your will. I want to experience the kind of transformation Martha did—moving from an earthbound attitude to a gracious heart filled with higher purpose. In Jesus' name, Amen.

JOURNALING

Take a few moments to record your personal insights from the lesson.

Her Uncompromising Commitment

CATCHING SIGHT
Introduction

*H*OW IMPORTANT IS it for us to keep a promise? Maybe a better question is how important is it for us that other people keep their commitment to us? When one couple's sons were young, the parents worked hard to teach them the importance of keeping their word. One of the boys wanted to join every sports team that came along. Often after joining, he would lose interest and want to quit after a few games. The parents would not allow him to quit but tried to teach him the importance of not letting the team down and the importance of thinking through a commitment before making it.

This lesson is about committing to a life of unwavering obedience. In *The Screwtape Letters* by C.S. Lewis, the demon Screwtape instructs a younger demon about ways to keep Christians from obeying the Lord. "Let him do anything but act. No amount of piety in his imagination and affections will harm us if we can keep it out of his will."[1] How very true! The enemy does not really care about our big plans as long as he can keep us from action.

Parents want their children to understand that delayed obedience is disobedience. Doesn't God want us to understand the same thing? How many times do we miss God's best in our lives when we lack the commitment to follow through on the plans we have for tomorrow? We will not be able to stand before God and say, "I intended to accept you; I intended to teach a Sunday School class; I intended to pray more; I intended to witness to my neighbor." Remember, delayed obedience is disobedience. God wants our uncompromising commitment to Him.

---

[1] C.S. Lewis, *The Screwtape Letters* (New York: Bantam Books, 1995), 39.

GETTING FOCUSED

Begin your study by sharing thoughts on this question:

What keeps us from fulfilling a commitment?

Bible Reading

Genesis 39:1–8; 20–23; Hebrews 11:22

New International Version	*New Living Translation*
Genesis 39:1 Now Joseph had been taken down to Egypt. Potiphar, an Egyptian who was one of Pharaoh's officials, the captain of the guard, bought him from the Ishmaelites who had taken him there.	Genesis 39:1 Now when Joseph arrived in Egypt with the Ishmaelite traders, he was purchased by Potiphar, a member of the personal staff of Pharaoh, the king of Egypt. Potiphar was the captain of the palace guard.
2 The Lord was with Joseph and he prospered, and he lived in the house of his Egyptian master. 3 When his master saw that the Lord was with him and that the Lord gave him success in everything he did, 4 Joseph found favor in his eyes and became his attendant. Potiphar put him in charge of his household, and he entrusted to his care everything he owned. 5 From the time he put him in charge of his household and of all that he owned, the Lord blessed the household of the Egyptian because of Joseph. The blessing of the Lord was on everything Potiphar had, both in the house and in the field. 6 So he left in Joseph's care everything he had; with Joseph in charge, he did	2 The Lord was with Joseph and blessed him greatly as he served in the home of his Egyptian master. 3 Potiphar noticed this and realized that the Lord was with Joseph, giving him success in everything he did. 4 So Joseph naturally became quite a favorite with him. Potiphar soon put Joseph in charge of his entire household and entrusted him with all his business dealings. 5 From the day Joseph was put in charge, the Lord began to bless Potiphar for Joseph's sake. All his household affairs began to run smoothly, and his crops and livestock flourished. 6 So Potiphar gave Joseph complete administrative responsibility over everything he owned. With Joseph there, he didn't

New International Version

not concern himself with anything except the food he ate.

Now Joseph was well-built and handsome, 7 and after a while his master's wife took notice of Joseph and said, "Come to bed with me!"

8 But he refused. "With me in charge," he told her, "my master does not concern himself with anything in the house; everything he owns he has entrusted to my care."

20 Joseph's master took him and put him in prison, the place where the king's prisoners were confined.

But while Joseph was there in the prison, 21 the Lord was with him; he showed him kindness and granted him favor in the eyes of the prison warden. 22 So the warden put Joseph in charge of all those held in the prison, and he was made responsible for all that was done there. 23 The warden paid no attention to anything under Joseph's care, because the Lord was with Joseph and gave him success in whatever he did.

Hebrews 11:22 By faith Joseph, when his end was near, spoke about the exodus of the Israelites from Egypt and gave instructions about his bones.

New Living Translation

have a worry in the world, except to decide what he wanted to eat!

Now Joseph was a very handsome and well-built young man. 7 And about this time, Potiphar's wife began to desire him and invited him to sleep with her. 8 But Joseph refused. "Look," he told her, "my master trusts me with everything in his entire household."

20 He took Joseph and threw him into the prison where the king's prisoners were held. 21 But the Lord was with Joseph there, too, and he granted Joseph favor with the chief jailer. 22 Before long, the jailer put Joseph in charge of all the other prisoners and over everything that happened in the prison. 23 The chief jailer had no more worries after that, because Joseph took care of everything. The Lord was with him, making everything run smoothly and successfully.

Hebrews 11:22 And it was by faith that Joseph, when he was about to die, confidently spoke of God's bringing the people of Israel out of Egypt. He was so sure of it that he commanded them to carry his bones with them when they left!

GAINING BIBLICAL INSIGHT
Committing to a life of unwavering obedience

A HIGH DIVER whose feet have just left the diving board provides a visual image which accurately defines the word *commitment*. The dive may take many forms from a highly stylized flip to a belly flop, but once the feet leave the board the diver is committed to the dive, having passed the point of no return.

Our studies thus far have brought us to the edge of the diving board. The topics we have discussed do not become personal realities until we make an uncompromising commitment to live by them.

A lasting Christian commitment will be based, first of all, upon the infallibility of the Word of God. The Bible is our guide for what we believe and how we live. Though attacked by critics through the years, the Bible still stands. In-depth biblical background studies of geography and archaeology only strengthen our understanding of the truth of God's Word.

In the Bible, we learn of people who made life-changing commitments to follow the Lord. One such person was Joshua who made the willful decision: "As for me and my household, we will serve the Lord" (Joshua 24:15). His firm decision to follow the Lord was modeled for him by his ancestor Joseph hundreds of years earlier in the land of Egypt. Joseph's uncompromising commitment is the subject of this study.

Commitment to God in Prosperity

Joseph lived in the patriarchal period before the Word of God was written. In this period God spoke directly to the patriarchs—Abraham, Isaac, and Jacob. God also spoke to Joseph, Jacob's son, through dreams which were a foreshadowing of his future. Joseph as a young man made a lifelong commitment to serve God.

Because Joseph talked about his dreams, his brothers became jealous and ultimately sold him into slavery in Egypt. However, the Lord prospered him (Genesis 39:2) and led him to a pleasant working environment. The household of Potiphar was blessed because of the presence of Joseph. Ultimately, Joseph became chief administrator of Potiphar's estate.

What challenges to commitment might Joseph have faced in this prosperous situation?

Apparently, prosperity did not change Joseph's commitment to serving God. When temptation arose, he was adamant in his resistance, seeing yielding to the situation as not only violation of his master's trust but also as sin against God (Genesis 39:9).

Commitment to God in Difficulty

Joseph's unyielding commitment led him from a prosperous position in Potiphar's household to confinement in prison, but Joseph maintained his relationship with God (Genesis 39:20,21).

What thoughts could have been going through Joseph's mind at this point?

In what difficult circumstances might our commitment to God be tested?

Which is easier, to serve God in prosperity or in difficulty?

Commitment to God in Spite of Disappointment

During Joseph's imprisonment, an occasion arose in which he interpreted dreams for two of his fellow prisoners, the king's baker and cupbearer. In both cases, the interpretations came to pass as Joseph said. The baker was hanged and the cupbearer delivered from prison. Joseph had requested that the cupbearer ask Pharoah to release him from prison. Two years went by with no action. These must have been two very long years for Joseph when he saw no deliverance coming from either man or God.

Disappointment with people may be a major threat to our commitment to serve God. We can become very vulnerable to discouragement when people let us down. But a greater disappointment may come when we feel God himself is not working on our behalf.

What do you think held Joseph steady through these two years?

What Scripture would you find helpful in a similar situation?

Commitment for the Future

The Book of Hebrews lists Joseph with the heroes of faith. In a brief account which mentions only one act of Joseph's faith, none of the actions we have studied are mentioned. The writer of Hebrews considers Joseph's instruction that his bones were not to be buried in Egypt as his greatest act of faith. This request identified him with the faithful servants of the Lord rather than with the pagan Egyptians.

Several hundred years later when Joshua led the nation, Joseph's bones were buried in Canaan (Joshua 24:32). Maybe carrying these bones through the wilderness gave Joshua time to think of the commitment it took to serve the Lord in adverse circumstances, and inspired him to make the same commitment himself.

Our commitment to Christ does not have ramifications for this life only. If we have placed our trust in Him, we have a future hope. This is the fulfillment of our faith and commitment. And perhaps our commitment will inspire future generations to follow in our steps.

In what way is your commitment to Christ an inspiration to others?

One such commitment was made by the young Mary who was chosen by God to become the mother of Jesus. When the angel came to her with the startling announcement that she had been chosen, she responded, "Let it be with me as you say." With those words she made a life-changing commitment to God's will.

REFLECTING HIS IMAGE
Mary (Luke 1:26–38; 2:1–7)

It's barely midafternoon and already I feel that today has been a long day. My feet are swollen and my lower back aches. Will this journey to Bethlehem never end? Joseph says we should arrive tomorrow late in the afternoon. This sweet donkey that carries us seems to know what precious cargo he is carrying. I see him step cautiously to avoid jarring the baby any more than is necessary. Joseph chose him carefully before we left home.

Nazareth seems like another world. My relationships with my family and friends will never be the same. In many ways, the events of past days still seem like a dream; one that I will awaken from soon. I was startled when the angel spoke to me. Humbled by his announcement. Does anyone completely understand about the prophesied virgin birth? I ask myself this question again and again. Even so, my answer was a simple, "Yes, I see it all now: I'm the Lord's maid, ready to serve. Let it be with me just as you say."[1] I know there is no turning back from this commitment.

It wasn't until I actually spoke of it to Joseph that it *sounded* real. Nothing seems real until I tell gentle, kind Joseph. How could I blame him for not being able to understand at first? Who am I that an angel should visit me? While Joseph loves me even though he couldn't actually believe what I told him, I am grateful that God gave him peace about the news in a dream.

With Joseph by my side, it doesn't matter what other people think. Oh, there are those "looks" we came to expect. After all, I face my family, friends, and community as an unmarried, pregnant woman. And pregnancy outside of marriage is just not tolerated in my town.[2]

But there is also the knowledge that we have been selected to be the parents of the Son of God, Yeshua—my baby—our son, God's Son. And through my moments of doubt and months of waiting while the child within me develops, I am learning every day to trust and praise God with our future.

It will take a lifetime to understand all of the miraculous events swirling around me, but in the meantime, I have a job to do—to raise the Son of God. No, I do not hesitate to trust God with my future.

My people have waited so long for the coming of Messiah. And now He is almost here. Will they accept that He is Messiah? Or will they not be able to see it as the prophets have said? I wonder.

It is time to get some food together for Joseph. I know he's concerned about a place for us to stay. He looks tired and anxious. But his voice is soothing to the donkey and to me. I know that God will show him the place for my baby to be born.

Abba Father, I worship You even more than I did on that day when the angel told me what was going to happen. I am truly humbled that You have selected me to be the mother of Your Son. There are things that I am not able to give Him. I cannot surround Him with wealth. I have little education. But I can give Him life, bone of my bone and flesh of my flesh. Until He is weaned, my warm milk will nourish Him. And along with Joseph, I

---

[1] Luke 1:38, *The Message.*
[2] *Voices of Faith,* 1309.

can give Him a home filled with love, trust, and understanding. Please God, may I always remember that while He is mine to care for, He will always belong to You.

EMBRACING THE PENTECOSTAL PERSPECTIVE
What is the Holy Spirit teaching me?

Mary's response to God's call—"I am the Lord's servant. May it be to me as you have said"—is a most amazing commitment (Luke 1:38). She listens to God's plan, asks one question, and agrees to God's plan! It sounds so simple, except that we know a multitude of reasons why Mary might have hesitated. The patriarch Joseph, son of Jacob, also showed us how to live a committed life in difficult circumstances. Is it possible for us to demonstrate commitment like that today? Absolutely!

Beyond the initial commitment to Christ as Savior, how has God called you to demonstrate your commitment to Him and to His Word?

What personal challenges do you confront in living out your commitment to Christ?

What kinds of barriers does the world construct to hinder your faith?

In the Old Testament, Joseph showed a commitment to serve God in prosperity and in prison, and in spite of disappointment, which led to the saving of an entire nation. Mary's decision to say "yes" to the Lord opened the door for the miraculous. The Holy Spirit would come upon her, causing her to conceive, and she would deliver the Savior. Jesus would live a sinless life, yet die for the sins of all, so that the world could be saved. Mary's commitment touches our lives today, as the commitments we make and live out will affect others now and in the future.

How does your commitment to family or friends resemble Mary's?

Does the way you live out your commitment to Christ carry consequences for the salvation of others? If so, how?

Do you rely on the strength the Holy Spirit gives to enable you to keep your commitment?

What miracles have you seen God do as a result of your commitment to pray, serve, believe, etc.?

How has your commitment stretched your faith?

Mary's commitment to carry God's Son was not something she could hide for very long. In an obvious way, her personal decision required public demonstration. Later, Jesus taught that the light of the world was not meant to be hidden (Matthew 5:14–16). Being open about one's relationship with the Lord is no easy task, especially when others are negative about your relationship. This relationship is not meant to be easy, nor is it meant to be undertaken in one's own strength. From the encouragement given by her cousin Elizabeth (Luke 1:41–45) to the inspiration that welled up within her (verses 46–55) to the reactions of others (2:18,19; 27–33), Mary was accompanied by the Holy Spirit.

Why do we sometimes fear people or their opinions more than we fear God?

Are you hiding your commitment to God from anyone in your life? Can you honestly say that you have openly shared Christ with everyone in your life?

How can you become a better encourager to fellow believers?

INVITING GOD TO CHANGE MY VIEW
What change is God asking me to make?

For this prayer time, break into smaller groups of two or three. In the privacy of personal conversation, share with your prayer partner(s) the situation weighing most heavily on your heart at this time:

- Have you made a commitment to Jesus, asking Him to be the Lord of your life?
- Have you compromised your faith with a bad decision?
- Do you desire a more demonstrative witness of your faith?
- Do you struggle with a perpetual area of compromise over which you want victory?
- Are you feeling isolated by a particular circumstance? Break the barrier by sharing your situation or asking for help.
- Has the Lord been dealing with your heart, asking you to follow Him in a new venture, but you have yet to indicate your willingness?
- Are there commitments you could make which would strengthen your faith?

Prayer
Father, I praise You for your uncompromising commitment to me. You have never failed me, never forsaken me, never changed. I can't say the same about this world, and I can't even claim to have come close myself. That's why I crave the fullness of Your Spirit in my life. I know my own weaknesses only too well. With Your Spirit, I can overcome anything that threatens my commitment to You. I want to make choices and live an uncompromising witness for You in this world. Strengthen me, Father. Quicken my senses to discern Your ways. In Jesus' name, Amen.

JOURNALING

Take a few moments to record your personal insights from the lesson.

Yours To Discover

Looking for Potential Inside Myself

_____

_____

_____

_____

_____

_____

_____

_____

_____

_____

_____

_____

Looking for Potential Inside Myself

_____

_____

_____

_____

_____

_____

_____

_____

_____

_____

_____

_____

_____

Looking for Potential Inside Myself

_____

_____

_____

_____

_____

_____

_____

_____

_____

_____

_____

_____

_____

Looking for Potential Inside Myself

_____

_____

_____

_____

_____

_____

_____

_____

_____

_____

_____

_____

Looking for Potential Inside Myself

_____

_____

_____

_____

_____

_____

_____

_____

_____

_____

_____

_____

Looking for Potential Inside Myself

_____

_____

_____

_____

_____

_____

_____

_____

_____

_____

_____

_____

_____

Looking for Potential Inside Myself

_____

_____

_____

_____

_____

_____

_____

_____

_____

_____

_____

_____

Looking for Potential Inside Myself

_____

_____

_____

_____

_____

_____

_____

_____

_____

_____

_____

_____

Looking for Potential Inside Myself

_____

_____

_____

_____

_____

_____

_____

_____

_____

_____

_____

_____

ARLENE ALLEN—Catching Sight

The teacup collection that she keeps is a testament to the Southern hospitality one receives when meeting Arlene Allen. Born in the Appalachian mountains of Virginia, she never fails to delight and challenge her audiences with her quick wit and Southern-style wisdom.

An ordained minister with the Assemblies of God, Arlene is the director for the national Women's Ministries Department. She serves on the boards of the national Women in Ministry Task Force, Religious Alliance Against Pornography, and Global Pastors' Wives Network. She has an extensive speaking history that includes pulpit ministry, leadership training, and women's and ministers' wives retreats.

Arlene has been married for thirty-nine years to Gary R. Allen who serves as the executive coordinator of the Ministerial Enrichment office of the Assemblies of God. The Allens are parents of two sons and the proud grandparents of two "incredible" grandsons, Grant and Jacob.

PEGGY MUSGROVE—Gaining Biblical Insight

In her new book, *Musings of a Maraschino Cherry,* Peggy Musgrove talks about the role of a pastor's wife as sometimes like being the cherry on top of an ice cream sundae. But her life and ministry has been far more than just mere decoration.

Peggy is a speaker and freelance writer. Previously, she served as national director of Women's Ministries for the Assemblies of God and director of Women's Ministries for the Kansas District Assemblies of God. Peggy's written works include *Who's Who Among Bible Women, Pleasing God, Praying Always,* and articles for several publications. Peggy holds two bachelor of arts degrees, one from Wichita State University and one from Central Bible College.

Peggy and her husband Derald served local churches and in district ministy in Kansas before moving in 1993 to Springfield, Missouri, where they both served in national offices for the Assemblies of God. They have two daughters, two "utterly awesome grandsons," and one "fabulously wonderful granddaughter."

When she's not writing, Peggy enjoys many things—reading, playing games, family holidays and vacations, spending time with her grandkids and friends, traveling with her husband, and antique shopping.

LORI O'DEA—Embracing the Pentecostal Perspective & Inviting God to Change My View

With discipleship being the passion of her ministry, Lori serves as the doctor of ministry coordinator and visiting professor of practical theology for the Assemblies of God Theological Seminary (AGTS). Previously, Lori served on pastoral staffs in churches in Decatur, Illinois, and Waterford, Michigan.

Lori was born and raised in Michigan and spent eight years in Illinois before relocating to her current home in Springfield, Missouri. She shares her home with her awesome cat, named Zipper, whom she claims can sail through the air like Michael Jordan. Aviation is one of her many interests and someday she would like to get her pilot's license. She's a firm believer that Mountain Dew, Doritos, and chocolate will be served in vast quantities at the Marriage Supper of the Lamb, though she has yet to find biblical support for her hopes.

Lori has spent a lot of time hitting the books and her educational credentials prove it. She earned a bachelor of science in missions and evangelism from Southwestern Assemblies of God University, her master of divinity with a dual emphasis in biblical languages and pastoral ministry, and a doctor of ministry in Pentecostal leadership from AGTS. In addition, Lori has served as a contributor to the *Complete Biblical Library* and *Enrichment Journal.*

CANDY TOLBERT—Reflecting His Image

She may have been transplanted to Missouri, but Candy Tolbert is a California girl at heart. She is a woman who "thinks out loud" about her love of God, love of spouse, love of children, and her passion for seeing other women reach their full potential in Christ. A licensed minister with the Assemblies of God for twenty-five years, Candy is the national leadership development coordinator for Women's Ministries.

Her extensive background includes public speaking, Christian education, missions, university student ministry, children's ministry, and music ministry. She has written articles appearing in the *Sunday School Counselor, Spirit Led Woman,* and *Woman's Touch* magazines.

Candy is married to the love of her life, Michael, to whom she has been married for twenty-five years. Together they pastored several churches in the Southern California area. Candy is also the proud mom of two daughters, Rachel and Ashley. Candy's other passions in life include home decorating and good coffee.

Unlimited potential to help you discover yours